MONEY SKILLS FOR MODERN TEENS

EMPOWER TEENS TO ACHIEVE LONG-TERM FINANCIAL INDEPENDENCE THROUGH THIS STEP-BY-STEP GUIDE TO ESSENTIAL MONEY SKILLS, INCLUDING BUDGETING, SAVING, INVESTING, AND MORE

PROSPERITY BOOKS

© Copyright 2024 - All rights reserved.

The content contained within this book may not be reproduced, duplicated or transmitted without direct written permission from the author or the publisher.

Under no circumstances will any blame or legal responsibility be held against the publisher, or author, for any damages, reparation, or monetary loss due to the information contained within this book, either directly or indirectly.

Legal Notice:

This book is copyright protected. It is only for personal use. You cannot amend, distribute, sell, use, quote or paraphrase any part, or the content within this book, without the consent of the author or publisher.

Disclaimer Notice:

Please note the information contained within this document is for educational and entertainment purposes only. All effort has been executed to present accurate, up to date, reliable, complete information. No warranties of any kind are declared or implied. Readers acknowledge that the author is not engaged in the rendering of legal, financial, medical or professional advice. The content within this book has been derived from various sources. Please consult a licensed professional before attempting any techniques outlined in this book.

By reading this document, the reader agrees that under no circumstances is the author responsible for any losses, direct or indirect, that are incurred as a result of the use of the information contained within this document, including, but not limited to, errors, omissions, or inaccuracies.

CONTENTS

Money Skills Roadmap

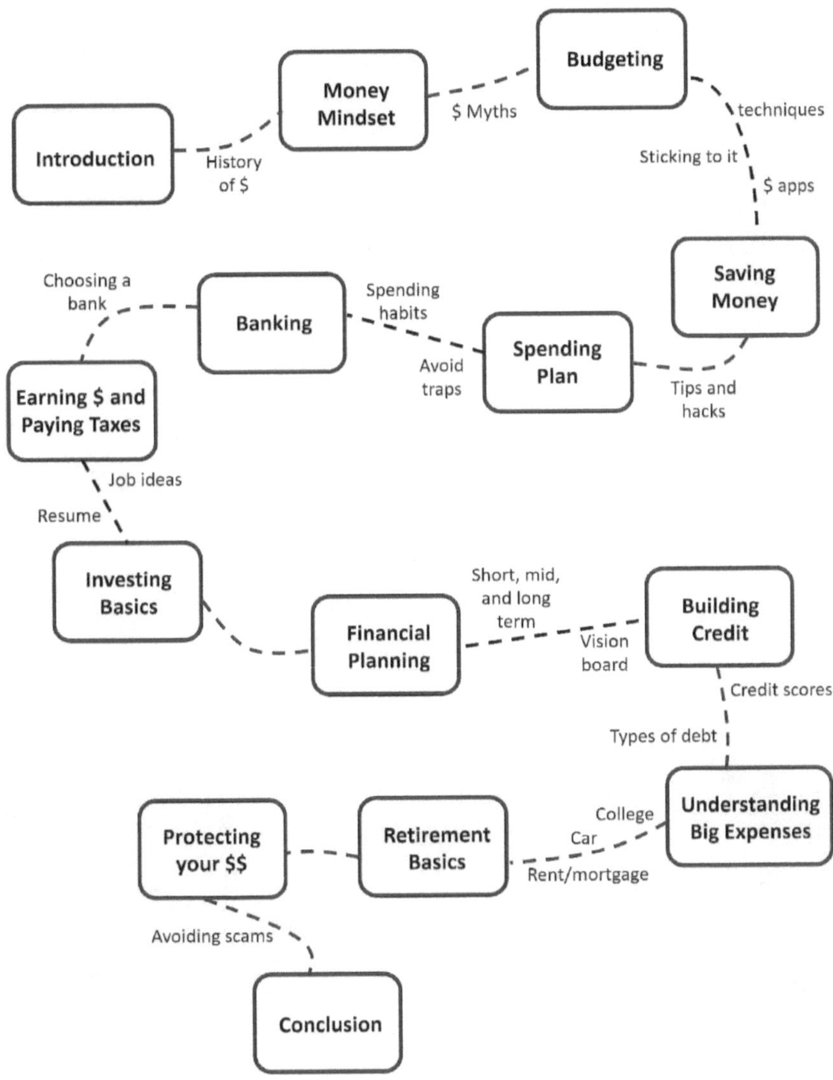

INTRODUCTION

If financial literacy is power, why do 75% of teens lack confidence in managing their finances (Turner, 2023)? But teens aren't the only ones having financial knowledge issues. Americans owe over $1.03 trillion in credit card debt alone (Dickler, 2023)! That's a lot! But who's to blame?

Well, most schools never explained how to do taxes or choose the correct bank account. Googling stuff like "What's a credit score?" just confuses most of us even more.

Looking back, I can totally relate! At 18, I constantly stressed about having enough cash to hang out with friends, buy clothes, and pay my phone bill. Money matters were boring to me. All I cared about was the freedom that came with being an adult.

But whoa... little did I know, with adulthood comes great responsibility, especially regarding money. For instance, the only thing I knew about banks was that they kept my money safe until I needed it back.

I know you can relate, too. We all have money questions that stress us out.

Maybe you want to save, but you can't overcome the temptation of spending little bursts of cash from gifts or part-time work. It feels so good—living in the moment. But this causes you to stress about money for bigger goals like concerts, college, or that gaming console.

Or maybe you're scared to even look at how much you've got in your account. The idea of managing budgets and bank services fries your brain. Trust me, I know!

WHY LEARN ABOUT MONEY?

You might wonder why you need financial skills downloaded into your brain. After all, you're young, with little income to manage now.

Here's the thing: Without money mastery, how can we fund the life adventures we crave... or even pay our phone bill on time? Financial literacy skills give us *freedom*. It means options and independence to chase our purpose—and have some Netflix binges, too!

It means that while some of your peers stress about penny-pinching and juggling multiple jobs to fund basic needs after high school or college, you can design a life around higher pursuits like passion projects, travel to exotic places, and starting an innovative business someday.

Doesn't that type of financial freedom sound way more fun to aim for? Money skills are about creating possibilities rather than limiting our potential.

That's why I insist on answering your most burning money questions now in simple, non-boring ways before you plunge into full adulthood! We'll cover questions like:

- What's the best way to make and manage income?
- How do smart saving goals work?
- When should I begin saving or investing?
- Which money apps can make things way easier?
- How do investing, taxes, and credit scores impact my future options?

And lots more!

THE PRIME METHOD

To accomplish our goal, we'll use my PRIME method—5 easy steps to transform your money mindset and hack financial literacy. It simply means:

Perceive: This deals with understanding the importance of being a financial guru in today's world.

Review: Through Chapters 2 to 4, you'll uncover how to take a step back, take in, and cross-check your plans, budget, savings, and expenses.

Invest: Investing is a way to earn money. From Chapters 5-7, we'll explore the world of investments and better understand banking services and taxes.

Mobilize: Here, you'll learn to finalize your game plan to achieve your life goals. Want to buy a house by 30? This is where you'll learn how to plan toward that.

Exercise: Knowledge without action is useless. In Chapter 11, you'll learn the best money practices.

With PRIME's guided money mindset shifts, you can ditch money stress for confidence and freedom before you know it. Imagine yourself in five years. What financial freedom dreams do you have? Visiting that dream island? Surfing the wild ocean? Building security for your family's future? Pursuing entrepreneurial ideas? I genuinely believe ANYTHING is possible with money mastery.

THE SWEET PERKS!

So, in this book, we'll keep things conversational—no lecturing! I'll answer your real money questions with many "ugh, been there!" stories and actionable money hacks.

For instance, you'll master:

- Budgeting and saving in savvy ways so you can enjoy small luxuries now, and powerfully grow money for epic future goals. Live boldly without going broke!
- Discovering the latest money apps and tools that make it effortless to pay friends, organize spending, and automate saving. Ditch money, boredom, and overwhelm!
- Having clever (and tricky) conversations around allowances, family support, and money mindset differences. Reduce awkwardness and gain freedom!
- Avoiding ouch-worthy mistakes regarding credit cards, filing taxes, and insurance needs. Save yourself major headaches down the road!
- Growing your income in alignment with skills and passions you already love pursuing. Make money moves much more fun!

With PRIME by your side, you'll quickly become the money master without stress!

ARE YOU READY TO TAKE CONTROL AND UNLOCK YOUR DREAMS?

Now, this isn't puffy rainbows talk here. I know money confusion and anxiety feel real right now at your age. But I promise—*freedom is achievable* if you commit each week to soaking up financial knowledge and mindset shifts with me on these pages.

How do I know? Because I've made plenty of money mistakes myself over the years. My slip-ups and emotional pitfalls taught me how to make this simple and *honest.*

So, my friend, stick with me through the chapters, and you'll become a full-fledged money expert all your friends admire!

The choice is yours. Will you look back in regret five years from now and wish you had taken control of your financial path starting today? Or will you grab the power, transformation, and possibilities for your wildest dreams that financial literacy provides? I can't wait to witness the incredible financial freedom you will achieve!

The possibilities for money mastery and freedom are endless when we commit fully. I can't wait to witness your a-ha moments and celebrate your wins! First step? Turn this page with me to begin gaining money superpowers!

CHAPTER ONE

MONEY MINDSET FOR SUCCESS

So, my happiness doesn't come from money or fame. My happiness comes from seeing life without struggle.

— NICKI MINAJ

Ever noticed how differently your friends treat money? Sam always spends money on V-bucks in Fortnite, hoping to level up holographic skins that all his squad mates obsess over. Emma uses her after-school job money to constantly buy the latest Disney+ merch and dress up for TikTok cosplay. And introverted Jordan just lets gift money pile up unused in Venmo because money stuff gives him anxiety. As you continue reading, envision these money personality examples playing out with your actual friends' names.

As you can see, people have very different attitudes and habits regarding money management. Where do you fall on the spectrum? Keep reading to understand more about "money mindsets" and how they impact your financial situation. But, before that: What does money really mean to you anyway?

BRIEF MONEY HISTORY

What is Money Anyway?

Did you know that goats, cattle, corn, and even giant rocks were once used as money? It's true! Money originated as a way to exchange items of value. I feel you, another history lesson sounds boring. We'll keep it quick, I promise!

Turns out money's a pretty new invention. Our ancestors relied on good old-fashioned bartering of resources, goods, and skills. For instance, farmers might exchange eggs for metal tools. This could get inconvenient, though, when two people don't have what the other wants. But you get the drift.

You see, money is a medium of exchange that people in a society widely accept as payment for goods and services, and repayments of debts.

When Was Money Invented?

So, who used money first in human history? Contrary to popular belief, paper money printed by governments is a relatively new invention.

Fun tip: The first physical coins were minted around 600 BCE in the region of Lydia, which is now part of modern-day Turkey (Beattie, 2022). These first standardized coins were a gold-silver alloy. Kings and the first merchant banks distributed the officially sanctioned coins.

Before we dive into money management, let's understand the evolution of money. Money has taken on many different forms throughout history. Here is a quick walk-through of how money has evolved:

Earliest Form of Money: The Barter System

Before today's money or coins, our ancestors relied on the direct trading of goods, crops, and skills. This was an informal favor exchange of "you scratch my back, I'll scratch yours." For instance, an ancient farmer low on metal tools might barter a healthy chicken to a blacksmith in exchange for fashioning a metal sickle. But this required finding someone who had what you needed and also wanted what you had to offer. See the problem?

Commodity Money

Money progressed beyond awkward bartering into using desirable commodities as symbolic currency. People assigned universal value to scarce or useful items like livestock, bushels of grain, fragrant spices, gemstones, and so on.

Rather than directly trading six sheep for a season's worth of grain, farmers could exchange the commodity's widely recognized value. This was much easier than lugging live animals to market! These early valuables functioned as *commodity currencies*.

Gold and Silver Trading

As civilizations advanced, commodity money transitioned to using precious metals, most importantly gold and silver. Scarce, yet abundantly desired, gold and silver became universal currencies.

The first gold coins date back to over 2,500 years in ancient Greece and India (Beattie, 2022). Due to metallic currency's durability and portability along trade routes, gold and silver defined money for a millennium until the adoption of paper notes and currencies only centuries ago.

Representative Money

Transporting heavy, precious metal currency became risky and inconvenient. So people started using more portable objects, like paper notes made from leather or wood. These objects represented an equal value of stored gold or silver.

For example, if I brought in 20kg worth of gold, they gave me an object—that served as a receipt—stating that I had 20kg worth of gold in store. This representation made transfers much easier than heavy gold or silver.

Gold Standard

Paper money had issues; it was becoming worthless. To solve this problem, governments set gold as the standard value of paper or coin money. For centuries, the value of paper and coin money was directly tied to the amount of physical gold held by ruling powers like monarchies or governments. This was called the gold standard.

For example, a $10 bill could theoretically be exchanged for $10 worth of real gold from reserves like *Fort Knox*.

Fun tip: *Fort Knox* currently holds almost half of America's stored gold. That's 147.3 million ounces (United States Mint, n.d.)!

This created a more "real" or tangible basis for money's worth. The gold standard prevailed globally by 1900, backing major currencies until the mid-20th century (Kumar, 2014).

Fiat Money

Formerly, money had real value in commodities like gold or was derived from its link to precious metals. However, gold was a scarce commodity, so it also led to more problems. Then came "*Fiat money.*"

Nowadays, money has value because governments declare it legal tender, not because it represents something tangible like gold. Most paper money today is "fiat money"—it derives its value from government ruling rather than physical commodities.

Digital Money and Cryptocurrencies

In the past, money meant having actual paper bills or coins stored somewhere to use later. You needed the physical money on you to spend it. Now, digital money allows money to be transferred instantly between people's accounts on their phones without needing the actual cash. Your money now lives as an online balance in apps like Venmo, CashApp or TikTok instead of a wallet. Unlike paper money that could be counterfeited before, there are more protections and tracking with digital transfers people can trust.

Maybe you've heard of cryptocurrencies. Maybe not. It's a revolution taking place right before our eyes!

Cryptocurrencies are new forms of digital currencies. Cryptocurrencies, like Bitcoin™, take transactions a step further by allowing direct exchanges online without banks or governments as intermediaries. Instead, these currencies rely on advanced computing algorithms to regulate their creation and use.

THE BANKING SYSTEM

The banking system consists of public centralized banks and private commercial ones that interact to manage money supply and availability.

Most countries have a centralized national bank that oversees the country's finances. For example, the U.S. Federal Reserve and the EU's European Central Bank. In addition, central banks don't deal directly with consumers, but their actions indirectly impact people's buying power.

Then there are private retail banks like *Chase*, *Wells Fargo*, and *Bank of America* that provide financial services directly to the public, you and I. Private banks handle accounts, transactions, lending, credit cards, and investments on a consumer level (chap. 5).

THE MOVE TOWARD CASHLESS SOCIETIES

The COVID pandemic led many places to rely more on credit cards, apps like Venmo, and other digital payments. Some even predict paper money could disappear as digital takes over.

Supporters think going fully digital could give governments more oversight to catch crooks. However, critics argue requiring all electronic payments introduces privacy questions and risks. What if the power, or the internet, fails?

Right now, most money in circulation still comes in physical paper bills and coins. This suggests people still prefer and trust the anonymity of cash.

But apps allow sending money super quickly and setting up accounts safely using your fingerprint or face login. For even greater security, banks let you protect your money by making you enter both special login codes texted to your cell and passwords to prove your identity. This double security check is referred to as *Two-factor Authentication*.

The trend seems headed toward more digital while still having physical cash options available. What's your take? Would you miss paper money if it went away? Or does it make you nervous only to have virtual dollars?

WHAT'S YOUR MONEY MINDSET?

Let's circle back to Emma from the opening. Her addiction to purchasing Disney merchandise and TikTok costumes leaves Emma always worried about where her next paycheck will come from. Even when she earns money, her shopping sprees never allow her to achieve any growth.

Anxious Jordan is left too overwhelmed to use his Venmo-gifted money because he avoids money management entirely. Because of this, Jordan misses out on concerts and gaming gear his friends enjoy. His anxiety also holds him back from saving for a car when he turns 16, something he has always dreamed about to gain more freedom and independence.

Each of them had a different *money mindset*. What is a money mindset? *Our money mindsets are subconscious beliefs about money's status, meaning, and role.* Our emotions and money-related values can also influence our financial habits, which impact how we manage our finances.

Our assumptions about money drive our behaviors, such as budgeting and debt management. Understanding that our emotions and money-related values can also influence our financial habits is crucial. In other words, having an education isn't enough; you must also change your mindset!

Do toxic attitudes limit your financial potential? Or does your money mindset set you up for success? By exposing flawed thinking, we can embrace empowering beliefs for prosperity.

Financial experts broadly categorize money mindsets into "good" or "bad." The thing is, your money mindset will shape how you deal with finances.

Good money mindsets lead to healthy financial choices and wealth accumulation over time. Bad money mindsets often result in money issues or constant financial struggles.

For example, here are some common types of "bad" money mindsets along with their downsides:

The Ostrich: The ostrich mindset is sticking one's head in the sand and ignoring money issues rather than budgeting or reviewing finances. This leads to surprise debt and financial hardship over time.

The Peacock: This is common on social media. It is the obsession with appearances, showing off flashy purchases for status without regard for costs/debt. Resulting in excessive spending and chronic debt issues.

The Miser: Being miserly and hoarding every penny due to money anxiety. Takes joy out of life and may still result in poor outcomes if money isn't invested.

Do any of the above sound familiar? To be honest, do you avoid budgeting? Post online to seem "rich"? Stress a lot about money? Most of us lean toward ostrich, peacock, or miser at times! Being aware of your money mindset alone can lead to progress.

On the other hand, here are examples of "good" money mindsets:

The Optimist: Staying positive and goal-focused when money is tight. Keeps you motivated toward prosperity rather than dwelling on temporary setbacks.

The Analyst: Thoroughly tracking every expense and income source to inform smart money strategies. Creates visibility allowing you to make control financial choices.

The Investor: Continuously learning about money and exploring ways to invest in yourself or ventures to achieve returns over time. Compounding gains build long-term wealth.

See the flip side? Where do you currently fall on the money mindset spectrum—fearful or successful thinking? Don't fret—with awareness and some dedicated work; you can re-frame your money mindset over time.

Our money mindset holds real power. It doesn't just shape our savings accounts but our outlooks, opportunities, and even relationships. An unhealthy mindset puts all of that at risk. The good news? With focused effort, our money mentalities can be transformed for good.

Our money mindsets develop early in life based on messages from parents, peers, school, and the media. For example, a child who observes parents anxiously fighting over expenses may grow up with emotional fears or trauma around finances. On the flip side, a child with parents who discuss budgets calmly may feel more confident with money matters.

Societal pressures and popular media also impact financial attitudes. Ever felt down scrolling through the social media feeds of your "friends" on glam shots traveling the globe or flaunting expensive outfits? The urge to keep up by overspending on the coolest gadgets and brands leaves many young people cash-strapped. These unrealistic standards fuel bad money mindsets.

Remember Po in Kung Fu Panda? He was raised by a noodle-cooking goose who told him pandas couldn't master martial arts. Po believed these self-limiting stories at first when he felt out of shape and talentless. However, his mentor, Master Oogway, spotted potential in Po that Po couldn't see for himself. To become the Dragon Warrior, Po must first shift his mindset to believe in his capabilities!

You may have absorbed faulty money myths growing up, too. But your financial destiny isn't fixed! You have loads of financial potential just waiting to be unlocked! Your money story is what you make of it.

Ready to transform your financial way of thinking? Here is a quick exercise to identify and upgrade your current money mindset:

Step 1: Grab a notebook and make three columns titled "Thoughts", "Feelings" and "Behaviors."

Step 2: Set a timer for 5-10 minutes. During that time, write down any money thoughts that pop into your head in the first column. Be brutally honest with yourself! Examples: "I'll never understand budgeting" or "I deserve nice things."

Step 3: In the second column, note the emotion or feeling that arises with each money thought. For instance, the thought "Budgets are boring" may spark a feeling of anxiety, frustration, or overwhelm.

Step 4: Finally, jot examples of financial behaviors that thoughts and feelings tend to trigger for you. "I avoid tracking spending because budgets make me anxious," for example.

Step 5: Now examine patterns between the three columns. Do certain unhelpful money thoughts keep resurfacing? Are the sabotaging behaviors leading to poor financial outcomes?

Use these insights to shift your inner money dialogue. For example, replace "Investing is too complicated for me" with "I'm eager to learn smart investment strategies." Doing this mental work will slowly transform your financial way of being!

BECOMING A FINANCE GURU

Cultivating a healthy money mindset marks a critical first step on your journey toward financial freedom, but mastering your inner money game is only part of the equation. You also need financial literacy: Concrete knowledge, skills, and competence in managing money.

Think of it this way: A peaceful, focused mindset serves as the solid foundation for building financial capability. With a firm base established, it's time to start sculpting knowledge and know-how through dedicated practice.

Let me tell you a story about why financial literacy is so critical...

A few years back, I received an unexpected windfall of $5,000 from a relative. At the time, I had two options—invest the cash into launching an online business I had been planning, or blow it all on a lavish vacation abroad.

I loved the idea of lounging on tropical beaches in a fancy resort for a week with friends, paying for it all. Without financial literacy guiding me, I was clueless about better uses for this money that could secure my future. So off, I jetted for a spontaneous vacation that was gone in a flash (and left me in debt after!).

In hindsight, investing that money into building solid income streams could have been life-changing. If only I had possessed the money management skills back then to make wiser financial choices!

Financial literacy is critical for making sound money decisions, avoiding rip-offs, and securing your future. Those with money smarts enjoy advantages like:

- higher income and net worth over a lifetime
- confidence making independent money moves
- preparedness for money challenges
- more options and opportunities
- peace of mind and life satisfaction
- clarity on personal spending habits and values
- passing on strong financial habits confidently

As Master Oogway says: "*There are no accidents*" (Goodreads, n.d.). Now that you've joined me on this financial journey, I promise you'll gain knowledge leading to life-long financial benefits!

Checkpoint

With Chapter 1 behind us, congratulations—you've completed the first step of our PRIME money makeover method: Perceiving personal money beliefs limiting your potential.

We learned historical forms of money leading to today's complex global economy. More importantly, you now recognize how ingrained mindsets shape financial outcomes.

After some reflection, you've identified your own inner money stories. And you're already changing self-talk to upgrade money beliefs! With this solid mental foundation now poured, get ready...

In the next chapter, we'll start applying financial power by managing spending and maximizing savings. I'll be right here when you're ready to continue our money mastery quest! *Remain calm, young panda; peace flows through you like...Ommmmm.*

CHAPTER TWO

STICKING TO A BUDGET

"A budget is not just a collection of numbers, but an expression of our values and aspirations"

— MARTIN, 2023

How true that rings for my neighbor's teenager, Jose. This 17-year-old burned money faster than California wildfires. Worse, he believed dangerous budget myths:

- *"Budgets are too restrictive—I need freedom!"* Jose felt budgets killed his vibe.
- *"Unexpected expenses always strike, so why bother budgeting?"* Healthy savings are boring to Jose.
- *"Budgeting means no more eating out. I hate cooking!"* Jose means to live the life.

Many of us hold similar myths about budgeting. And what are the outcomes of holding onto such beliefs? I tell you... very predictable: mounting debt, bitter arguments with parents over money, little savings, and difficulty envisioning bigger goals like college or moving out.

Ever witnessed such situations? It's pretty common. Sadly, Jose is not alone in such a financial no-man's land. According to a 2019 Lincoln Financial Group survey, over 67% of Americans do not maintain a personal budget (Marder, 2023). Remember I said holding bad budgeting myths results in mounting debt? Well, a 2022 CNBC report revealed that over 60% of Americans live paycheck to paycheck. In addition, most people waste as much as $3,000 per year (Dickler, 2023b).

It's wise to learn from history and not repeat the same mistakes.

My young friends, shed those damaging money myths! A budget aligns spending with values and can prevent $3,000 average annual waste. This chapter will debunk budget falsehoods for good. Get those spreadsheets ready as we dive into the fundamentals. Budgeting can be fun and rewarding if you stick with it—I promise!

THE ESSENCE OF A BUDGET

What exactly *is* this seemingly dull yet critical money management tool called a "budget"? At its core, a budget is simply a plan for spending and saving money. I like to think of it as a checklist guiding how every dollar earned will be used. Sure, an occasional surprise expense may come up. But with good planning, you can account for those too.

How does the budget work? It lets you take charge of expenses through:

- tracking all income streams; dollars coming in
- categorizing exactly where every dollar goes, that is, expenses
- optimizing limited money across all needs and desires

Alright, now, let's break down the major components of the budget:

- **Income:** All sources of money coming in, whether a regular allowance, income from a job or side hustle, gifts, and so on. This part of the budget helps us know exactly what is available to fund spending.
- **Savings:** Pay yourself first before spending on anything else! Saving money requires a conscious effort for non-essential goals on limited budgets and keeps your financial goals on track.
- **Necessities:** The non-negotiable things needed for daily living like housing, utilities, groceries, transportation, minimum debt payments, insurance, and so on.
- **Unrestricted spending:** Everything else is not essential! Things like hobbies, entertainment, eating out, and so on. Budget a set amount for these wants each month.
- **Debt payments:** If paying down debt, budget the exact monthly payment amount beyond the minimum due. List each debt balance separately so you know what needs tackling.

A basic budget table would look something like this:

Sources of income	Amount earned
Job Salary	$2,000
Parent Allowance	$150
Summer Pet Sitting	$200
Total Income	**$2,350**

The table above records all sources of income.

Expenses categories	Date	Amount
A. Necessities		
1. Groceries		
2. Water bill		
3. Gas		
Total		
B. Entertainment		
4. Netflix subscription		
5. Social hangouts		
Total		
C. Savings		
6. College funds		
7. Concert		
8. Emergency funds		
Total		

You can expand on the above to include more items. The goal is to capture every cash in-flow (Income) and out-flow (Expenses).

BUDGETING TECHNIQUES

Alright, my money ninjas, it's time to master the secret art of budgeting! Yes, there are actually different flavors and styles when it comes to making and sticking to a budget. Don't worry; I'll break down the most powerful techniques for you step-by-step. We've got the intensity of Zero-Based Budgeting, the simplicity of the Envelope System, and the classic balanced 50/30/20 Budget.

Zero-Based Budgeting

This intense budgeting method will have you feeling like a financial martial arts master. That's because, with Zero-Based Budgeting (ZBB), you start from zero each month and carefully assign every single dollar you earn to a specific purpose. Nothing gets left hiding out for random expenses to gobble up!

Follow these steps to put ZBB in action:

1. **Record total monthly net income:** First, calculate your total take-home pay after taxes and deductions. Be sure to include all sources if you have a side income, gift money, etc.
2. **Assign dollars to fixed expenses:** Make a master list of recurring essential expenditures like rent, car insurance, groceries, and minimum loan payments. Budget dollars to cover each upfront.
3. **Allocate money to financial goals:** Figure your monthly amounts needed to meet targeted savings levels and additional debt repayments. Assign dollars accordingly.
4. **Budget for lifestyle expenses:** With money left after funding needs and goals, decide on a monthly fun money allowance for dining out, entertainment, hobbies, etc.

5. **Adjust to reach total income:** If assigned expenses and savings don't equal your full pay, make cuts to unnecessary spending until the total balance.

ZBB takes effort but guarantees you control every dollar wisely. Use an Excel sheet or budgeting app (list soon) to track and adjust categories easily. The benefit of Zero-Based Budgeting is that it gives your dollars purpose through careful planning. Just beware of getting overwhelmed trying to manage every single dollar!

Image with permission of Piscine on iStock

The Envelope System

If intense detail isn't your thing, the envelope system may be your budgeting style. This easy, old-school technique has you setting up actual envelopes to hold cash for certain spending categories. Here's how it works:

1. **Label envelopes by spending category:** Write category names like "Groceries," "Gas," "Clothes," "Dining Out," and so on. Create an envelope to represent each regular expense.

2. **Assign cash to each:** Based on typical monthly expenditures, withdraw cash after each paycheck to evenly distribute among envelopes.
3. **Spend only from assigned envelopes:** When you need to spend in a certain category, use only the amount available in the matching envelope. No "borrowing" or overspending allowed!
4. **Adjust monthly additions If needed:** Avoid constantly running envelopes dry before the month ends. Exercise restraint or put more aside next month for problem categories.

When an envelope is empty, you cut off spending in that category until next month. This system is super simple and hands-on. The only risk is losing an actual envelope of money!

Image with permission of Henderson Jr on iStock

The 50/30/20 Budget

Finally, we have the balanced budgeting icon: the 50/30/20 system. This budgeting style takes the commonly recommended spending guidelines and makes them easy to follow. Simply:

- **50% to necessities:** Housing, transportation, groceries, minimum loan payments, and other basic needs.
- **30% to lifestyle:** Dining out, entertainment, hobbies, electronics, or other non-essentials.
- **20% to savings and extra debt repayment:** Emergency fund, retirement contributions, early mortgage/loan pay-offs.

You want to ensure you:

- *calculate* monthly net income
- *categorize all expenses* and tally totals for needs vs. wants
- *adjust spending to meet targets*
- *re-balance periodically* as income and obligations change over time

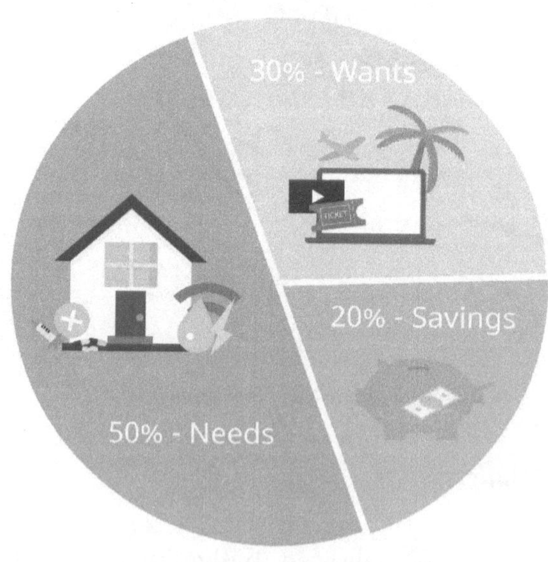

Image with permission of Piscine on iStock

Confusing? Don't worry; here's an example of how it's done.

Say Emma earns *$4,000 per month* after taxes as a graphic designer. Using the simple 50/30/20 allocation, here is what her monthly budget would look like:

1. Emma's total monthly net income is $4,000.

2. 50% of Emma's income is $2,000 (50% x $4000). This $2,000 must go toward Needs like:

- Rent: $1,200
- Car payment and insurance: $350
- Groceries and home supplies: $300
- Utilities: $150
- **Total needs** = $2,000

3. 30% of Emma's $4,000 is $1,200 (30% x $4000) for her Wants. This will cover expenses like:

- Restaurants and bars: $400
- Shopping and entertainment: $300
- Gym membership: $40
- Streaming services: $20
- Video editing course: $440
- **Total wants** = $1,200

4. Finally, 20% of $4,000 is $800 (20% x $4000) for Savings and Extra Debt Payments:

- Retirement contribution: $300
- Student loan over-payments: $200
- Building emergency fund: $300
- **Total savings and extra debt** = $800

By strictly budgeting based on the 50/30/20 income percentages, Emma ensures she takes care of her needs and financial goals first before spending freely on wants each month.

Since targets are already set, the 50/30/20 style takes less planning. However, you need the income to actually support saving 20% if you hope to reach your financial goals responsibly!

LET'S BUDGET!

Alright, money masterminds, it's time to put your newfound budgeting knowledge into action! You learned about 3 different methods: Zero-Based, Envelope, and 50/30/20 budgeting. Try formulating your own personal budget using any of the mentioned techniques.

Once you finish setting up your chosen style of budget, carefully look it over and determine:

- Are fixed living expenses fully covered?
- What about financial goals like emergency savings contributions?
- How much is going toward non-essential fun spending? Too much? Too little?

A budget is just a guide that you will likely need to adjust over time as income or expenses change. The key is sticking with your monthly money framework. Test-drive your new budget to track progress and then re-evaluate in 3 months. Tweak category amounts as needed!

STICKING TO A BUDGET

Making your budget work long-term boils down to making it manageable and setting up structures that encourage compliance. Here are 9 solid tips:

1. **Automate payments and transfers:** Automate payments and transfers so that contributions to needs, savings goals, and debt happen seamlessly each month. Set up automatic drafts through your bank account or paycheck direct deposit, using bill pay services or money apps like *Mint*.

2. **Use accountability partners and budgeting apps:** Use accountability partners and budgeting apps like *Mint, You Need a Budget, Personal Capital,* or *EveryDollar* to monitor category spending closely (more on these soon).

3. **Organize budget to fit your lifestyle:** Find an organization system that fits your lifestyle, whether that's a simple spreadsheet or an intricate money management journal. Categorize expenses in a way that makes sense to you for easy tracking.

4. **Side hustles:** Look for ways to earn side income via a weekend side hustle or launching an *Etsy shop* if your main income makes your budget feel overly tight or restrictive month to month. Exploring untapped profit potential gives you more money flexibility (See Chapter 6).

5. **Save the big purchases for later:** Practice delaying big purchases to test if wants are just impulsive or worth the trade-off. Sit on the decision for a few days and see if the desire remains strong. Often, with time, the thrill passes— saving your budget!

6. **Involve parents/family/roommates:** Make living mates aware of your budget categories, especially shared costs

like utilities, streaming services, or household supplies. Prevent surprise overages together.

7. **Always go shopping with shopping lists:** Build meal plans and shopping lists to resist restaurant and grocery splurges. Map out recipes for the week and compile ingredients needed, then stick to them without tossing extras in the cart hostage to cravings!

8. **Reward yourself:** Schedule intentional and affordable treats that align with your goals (like a pedicure when you hit 1 month sticking to the budget). Build in reasonable rewards that incentivize you to stay on track.

9. **Celebrate your budgeting milestones:** Take some time out to celebrate your success. Enjoy free—but planned and budgeted—window shopping trips, picnics in the park, game nights, or library book binges. You feel just as fulfilled without blowing the budget.

TOP BUDGETING APPS

Remember when I mentioned that budgeting apps could smoothly balance your money like a money ninja? Well, it's time to showcase apps to help you budget with power! I'll break down the features of leading picks:

EveryDollar

Crafted by finance guru Dave Ramsey, The *EveryDollar* app rules for its simple design, encouraging messages, and making Zero-Based Budgeting easy. Highlights include:

- intuitive interface for all budgets
- set savings goals and bill alerts
- mobile access across devices

- syncs with bank accounts
- family sharing upgrades

With the ability to rate spending priority and get alerts before overspending, *EveryDollar* keeps the budget on lock. Download the must-have app for free!

PocketGuard

PocketGuard eliminates cash flow confusion through machine smarts. It automatically sorts transactions into budgeted categories without tedious manual entry. So you get effortless money insights like:

- projected account balances
- custom categories and reporting
- recurring subscription detection
- bill pays through the app
- surprise charge alerts

Take the work out of figuring out where that mystery $100 went each month with *PocketGuard*! The app is free, but premium upgrades are available.

GoodBudget

For hands-on helpers, *Goodbudget* budgeting emulates the envelope system through digital tools. Enjoy features like:

- colorful virtual envelopes
- group sharing for couples/families
- easy importing of transactions
- budget snapshot dashboard

- tablet and desktop access, too

Stick to your spending money limits without losing actual cash-stuffed envelopes. Download *Goodbudget* free on smartphones or with one-time software purchases for larger screens.

REVIEWING AND ADJUSTING YOUR BUDGET

Budgets evolve as life changes: What works today might need some tweaks tomorrow. Reviewing your money road map quarterly lets you ensure things are still on track.

When to Review

Aim to formally revisit your budget 3-4 times yearly with your tax return, mid-year, early Fall for holiday planning, and so on. You'll likely need sporadic monthly check-ins, too, if unexpected events hit.

What to Look For

Assessing these 3 factors ensures your budget still aligns with financial realities:

Income: Did any amounts decrease through job loss or pay changes? Or did they increase via raises/bonuses or gifts? Extra summer break gig?

Expenses: Which spending needs to be spiked or lessened? Utilities, debt payments, and insurance tend to fluctuate. Very rarely do costs stay completely static.

Goals: Have priorities changed regarding things like debt payoff, vacations, and home ownership? When life happens, adjust the time frame or your monthly savings contributions accordingly.

HOW TO UPDATE

Carefully re-work affected categories using the latest totals. Move any extra dollars toward goals in need of a boost.

Let's walk through how high school junior Akira would review and change her budget when life events happen.

Akira gets paid $100 weekly at her part-time job. She tries to put $50 per paycheck toward a used Jeep. But with senior year approaching, Akira realizes she needs to bump up her savings for prom expenses coming soon.

Here's how Akira adjusts her budget the easy way:

1. Akira reviews her income, and it's steady at $400 a month.
2. She notes expenses rose only $20 for a music streaming subscription.
3. Akira evaluates her goals and decides to increase prom fund contributions from $30 to $50 weekly.
4. Using her budgeting app, Akira immediately allocates the extra $20 each paycheck to prom savings.
5. The app automatically reduces her "Jeep fund" category to make up for the difference.

Just like that, Akira's budget redistributes dollars to match her current top priority—painlessly, thanks to her digital system updating everything automatically. She can revisit goals again next semester if needed.

Updating your money plans doesn't have to be scary or confusing, despite life's curve balls. Pick a quarterly checkpoint and follow Akira's lead!

Checkpoint: Budgeting Session Over!

Great job getting through the budgeting boot camp! Let's recap key lessons real quick:

Budgeting benefits: A budget aligns income with spending priorities for stability. You dictate dollars; they don't rule you!

Budgeting strategies: Choose a method matching needs—from detailed Zero-Based to simple 50/30/20 allocation. Envelopes work too!

Budgeting tools: Apps like *EveryDollar*, *PocketGuard*, and *Goodbudget* make balancing easy through automation. Rely on tech!

Budgeting adaptability: Review quarterly and roll with life by first shifting money to essentials and savings. Build cushion space for volatility!

Stick within the budget's money guardrails and watch your accounts grow rather than randomly disappearing every month. Follow your budget and see compounded returns over time from cost-cutting and investing the rest for goals!

You're now a Budget Boss, and the next level is rapidly approaching! Up ahead, we tackle how to save effectively. Ready grasshopper? Then let's hop to it!

CHAPTER THREE
SAVING MONEY ON ANY BUDGET

"Predicting rain doesn't count. Building arks does"

— *BRAINY QUOTES*, N.D.-B

Investing guru Warren Buffett preached that stashing away part of your paycheck arms you for rainy days ahead. Yet today, only 1 in 4 teens actively save anything. I get it. Endless shopping temptation is shoved in our faces 24/7. But come on, you're smarter than that!

Check this: 60% of full-blown adults don't have $400 spare cash for emergencies without borrowing. Yikes! But by learning money truths early, we get to blaze brighter paths.

Yet inspiring hope exists! Take Kristina Ellis, who launched a babysitting business and disciplined savings at 17 to pay her own college tuition debt-free! Through stories in this chapter, we'll meet former financial train wrecks who turned things around through small yet consistent money actions over time.

The key is understanding compound interest—how small savings can grow exponentially when prudently invested over years or decades. We'll unlock this magic formula soon!

As part two of our proven *PRIME* method emphasizes, let's objectively *review* our current saving approach. *No matter how challenging things seem now,* I'll provide tips to start small yet think big. Tiny, consistent money actions snowball into sweet freedom—trust the process! We so got this!

WHAT ARE SAVINGS?

Simply put, savings means choosing not to spend every single dollar from your paycheck or gift money today. It's about storing value for when you need or want stuff later.

This gives your cash time to grow quietly thanks to something banks provide called "interest" (a cut for lending your dough to others). Park in investment accounts patiently; interest compounds over time.

Regardless of the method, saving creates options! Emergencies, wishes, dreams... you name it. Want a killer computer to launch that YouTube channel? Saving allows you to keep an eye on the prize 'til you can snag that sweet gear. Dig?

Peep this cheat sheet visualizing the main "savings buckets" out there:

Emergency Funds

An emergency fund is money set aside to cover unexpected costs life throws at you, like urgent medical bills, car repairs, or replacing a cracked phone screen. The goal is to have 3-6 months of your usual spending money tucked away for life's unpleasant surprises without needing to panic, dip into other funds, or go into debt. For example, if you spend around $100 a week on food, clothes, or hanging with friends, aim to ultimately save $1,200-$2,400 in a safe spot, like a high-yield savings account. Even starting with $5-10 per month builds security.

Retirement Accounts

This is covered extensively in Chapter 10.

College Funds

Higher education is increasingly vital for securing high-quality careers, yet it can be incredibly expensive. College graduates today average nearly $30,000 in student loan debt. Experts recommend saving and investing expressly for college using state-sponsored 529 plans to avoid borrowing. These feature valuable tax advantages that maximize growth. Consistently contributing even modest sums over your academic journey can yield serious tuition fund coverage!

Planned Purchases

We all have major one-time expenses on the horizon, maybe a coveted gaming laptop, study abroad semester, or a used car. Creating targeted savings funds earmarked explicitly for these bigger items allows us to enjoy guilt- and debt-free. Otherwise, impulse spending temptations might derail us from ever reaching those goals we deeply desire. Patience pays off!

Dream Goals

Finally, don't ignore your aspirational saving just because society considers certain ambitions "impractical" for those starting out! There are teens already well on their way to riches precisely by compartmentalizing small auto-deposits toward groundbreaking ventures, bucket list adventures, or philanthropic initiatives over long time-frames. Define what wildly transforms the world for you, then incrementally build the economic runway to get there. The sky's the limit!

Health Savings Accounts

A health savings account (HSA) is a special bank account that lets you save money just for medical expenses, tax-free. You can use these special savings set up specifically to cover health expenses down the road—whether next year or decades into retirement.

Contributing regularly to an HSA, even in small amounts, creates tax savings today while letting that money grow exponentially without any fancy Wall Street investing know-how. Then, later down the line, you'll have ample funds to handle medical bills without breaking a sweat.

WHY SAVE MONEY?

Consider this alarming statistic—40% of Americans can't cover a mere $400 emergency expense without borrowing money or selling something (Board of Governors of the Federal System, 2021). That means 4 in 10 adults stand one surprise crisis away from cascading turmoil.

Imagine the fallout if an urgent situation happened, but you lacked accessible savings. Perhaps the transmission in your only family car unexpectedly gives out... or an ER visit after a sporting injury drains several paychecks.

The lack of *channeled* cash reserves increases hardship during financial crises—often forcing desperate decisions with lasting consequences. Studies show that 70% of us suffer moderate to extreme anxiety when living paycheck to paycheck without savings to tap into should an emergency strike (Epperson & Dhue, 2023).

I'll never forget the palpable concern watching COVID lockdowns unfold with my teenage niece Ally years back. She *glances up from her phone, worried...*

"What's the problem?" I asked.

Ally: I'm feeling super stressed about money lately. Between college savings, unexpected medical bills, and everything else so uncertain, even with graduation ahead, it just feels impossible to get ahead!

Me: I hear you, kiddo. Honestly, I've been there, too—life throws crazy curveballs! But what if I told you saving money can help with all of that? Building up even small reserves provides freedom to handle almost anything.

Ally: Wait, really? How's some cash stashed away going to give me freedom?

Me: For starters, you gain independence to make choices rather than desperation forcing decisions. Then security, knowing you've got backup options...

Ally: Hmm, I think I'm following. But how would I actually start saving when expenses feel overwhelming as is?

Me: It's about priorities, not amounts. Pay yourself first automatically, even $5 or $10 from each check. Small, consistent actions compound faster than you think! Over time, you'll sleep better, too.

Niece: So not only do I get financial options, but also peace of mind from saving? I have to admit that sounds really good...

Me: Precisely! And don't forget, the more you save, the earlier money starts working for you through interest and investing. Making your money, make money! Then doors really start opening...

Ally: Wow, I never realized saving gave all that! Feeling motivated now... Thanks!

SAVING GOES BEYOND EMERGENCY

Aside from stacking up savings for emergencies, college, and other unexpected expenses, it could also be channeled to other endeavors such as:

Weathering Unemployment's Storm

Consistent savings enable us to endure better unforeseen circumstances, like job loss or income disruption. Consider Juan, who worked part-time as a barista, saving $75 from each paycheck while attending community college classes. When the coffee shop abruptly shut down due to the pandemic, Juan was concerned but grateful to have a few months' reserves to pay bills while finding another job.

We know that most people live paycheck to paycheck. Imagine the terror if we suddenly lose our only source of income—our nine-to-five. How do we survive? What do we eat? How do we pay rent?

Worrisome, right? Yes. If we can save just 6 months' worth of normal living expenses, then the impact of job loss is reduced. Plus, you are able to focus on getting another job. It's a win-win!

Turning Cents into Cold Hard Cash

Investing small amounts consistently over long time frames allows the *power of compound growth* to work its magic. Let's run some numbers to see the power of consistency and time. Simply saving $50 monthly at a modest 5% annual interest rate over 6 years results in over $4,000 earned rather than just the $3,600 physically saved—an extra $400+ boost! Now imagine doubling the monthly savings to $100... that's over $8,000 cumulatively after 6 years, thanks to compound growth!

If you saved the money in a piggy bank, you wouldn't earn any interest. This graph shows the free interest you would earn with each saving scheme above! I love free money, don't you?

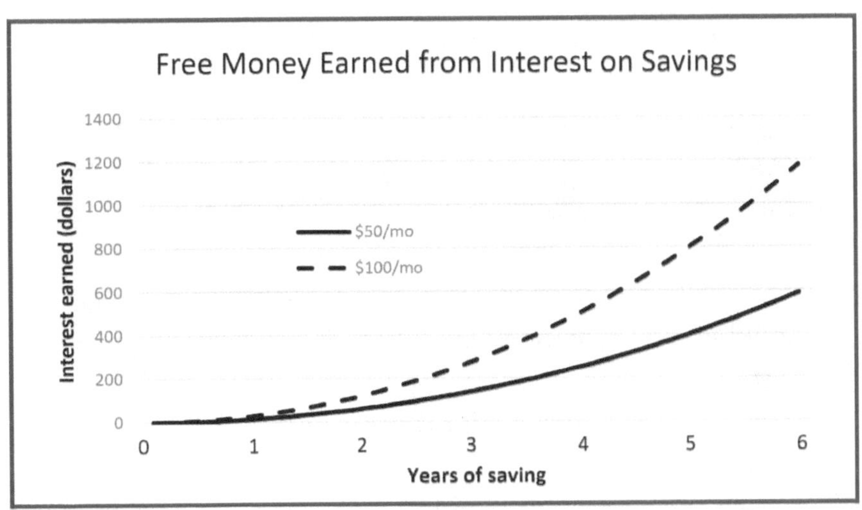

SAVINGS TIPS AND HACKS: TWELVE FAST WAYS TO SAVE MORE MONEY NOW

Managing money better doesn't mean we must sacrifice joy or lifestyle. We can discover ample savings opportunities in our everyday student lives with creative thinking and minor habit adjustments. I've compiled 12 fast, practical techniques for spending smarter, tailored to teens like you!

1. Automatically transfer part of any income into savings to start building value immediately.
2. Take turns sharing streaming subscriptions with friends to save money.
3. Round up purchase amounts to the next dollar and deposit the change into savings.
4. Use early bird discounts to save money and get home faster.
5. Check used item shops first before buying new items to save big.
6. Learn to negotiate respectfully for better deals on purchases.
7. Find cheaper alternatives like public transit that still meet needs.
8. Earn rewards in a savings account for skipping small splurges.
9. Carry only cash to encourage more thoughtful spending.
10. Split bulk item packs with family and friends to lower costs.
11. Use apps to sell unwanted stuff from home for commission.
12. Brown bag homemade food instead of buying meals out.

These bite-sized, no-commitment-required tips demonstrate that small, consistent actions across purchases, activities, and choices can quickly multiply into serious extra savings. When regularly applied, they provide the fuel for reaching our personal finance goals faster while still enjoying the perks of youth!

WHY SAVING MONEY EARLY IS IMPORTANT

Sure, we could wait a few more years before worrying about money management, right? But scientific research reveals that our financial behaviors—good and bad—start becoming wired early on. So seizing this formative window for positive habits pays dividends our whole lives!

Think of it like nutrition and fitness. Youth who consistently maintain healthy diets and activity levels tend to carry improved trajectories, avoiding obesity and disease pitfalls, compared to those not establishing healthy routines during developmental stages. The same goes for saving!

Early on, small amounts go far thanks to the power of compound growth over long time horizons. By diverting just $30/month during 4 years of high school, we could accumulate over $5,000 for jump-starting adult milestones like first cars, college costs, or apprenticeship training!

Savings habit Start Age	13 years old	17 years old
Monthly Savings Amount	$30	$30
Number of Years Saving	4	4
Total Savings Contributed	$1,440	$1,440
Assumed Annual Interest Rate	5%	5%
Total Interest Earned	$736	$576
Total Savings Plus Interest	**$2,176**	**$2,016**
Value Difference	-	**$160 less**

Top Teen Savings Apps

Managing money looks wildly different in 2023, courtesy of secure finance and technological (fintech) innovation, making automated savings seamless no matter our income levels. I've compiled insights on 3 leading solutions receiving sky-high praise for simplifying wealth building tailored to teens like you:

The table below shows key capabilities, value-added features relevant to students, built-in parental safeguards, and credibility backed by rave peer reviews. Whether automatically saving allowances, generating cash-back rewards, or effortlessly building investment portfolio value through round-ups—such technology empowers our financial potential.

Fintech App	Mvelopes	Current	Qapital
Description	Digital envelope budgeting system and financial planner	Top digital bank for teens seeking financial independence	Unique savings rules system to effortlessly build wealth
Key Features	Goal setting, spending triggers analysis, auto-transfers	Build credit and savings, guardian transparency on transactions	Round-ups, "Spend Guilt-Free" bucket strategies
Credibility (Reviews)	800+ reviews, averaging 4.5/5 stars	75,000+ verified 5-star reviews	75,000+ 5-star iOS and Android app store reviews
Pricing Plans	Basic $6/month, Premier $10/month with insurance	Totally free checking, savings, debit card	Free Core plan, $6 and $12 monthly premium plans
Parental Oversight	Moderate controls and account visibility	Full visibility into teen transaction activity	Limited controls but family sharing enabled

Small, consistent actions compound substantially over the years. Seemingly minor sums become thousands socked away for game-changing opportunities ahead. Delayed gratification wins the race. Luck meets preparation through progressing from nickels to the nest egg. Wield 21st-century applications *prudently as tailwinds, not headwinds*. Spend on needs to free up income for wants. Sacrifice neither. So, start now and smile later as sustainable saving snowballs over time!

End-of-Chapter

We've covered expansive ground explaining the manifold merits of cultivating diligent lifelong savings habits early on as the foundation for financial health and stability.

Whether protecting against surprise expenses through rainy day reserves, fueling aspirational purchases via targeted goal-sinking funds, or simply harnessing the unparalleled power of compound growth over long time frames—learning to set aside income to outperform spending consistently is a pivotal ritual on the path toward prosperity.

We tactically highlighted everything from psychological savings hacks to optimized mobile apps promising to ease and accelerate wealth creation; the broader principles resonate universally:

1. Start early and small, persistently.
2. Automate transfers whenever possible.
3. View savings as untouchable assets compounding value.
4. Patience and discipline over short-term indulgences.

Armed with essential knowledge for constructing personalized saving systems as step two of our PRIME methodology, let's carry positive momentum into strategically reviewing spending habits to amplify our financial capabilities further!

I will walk alongside you to translate aspirational budgets into realistic blueprints, balancing vital needs with responsible wants, and increasing investment deposits. Remember, every dollar intelligently saved today is two, then ten, then a hundred dollars more we can individually control tomorrow.

Onwards and upwards, my friends! Turn the page as we master the art of spending.

CHAPTER FOUR

MONEY PRIORITIES AND CREATING A SPENDING PLAN

"We buy things we don't need with money to impress people we don't like."

— DAVE RAMSEY

I stumbled across that quote while scrolling late one sleepless night, and it stopped me in my tracks. I had just blown most of my birthday money on concert tickets with people who weren't my close friends.

Surveys show over 50% of teenagers harbor regrets about similar impulsive purchases (Gillespie, 2023). Bummer? But we've all been there, seeing something totally cool on *Instagram* or *Snapchat*, buying it without thinking, and then realizing we wasted money trying to impress people who don't really care.

But get this: You'll feel way happier if you spend money on stuff within your budget that matches your real priorities as opposed to spending irresponsibly. This chapter contains tips to categorize expenses, see if they align with your values, and build a flexible custom money plan for where you're at.

The big idea is finding the right combo of spending, saving, and giving back that works for you. We all feel pressured to buy stuff online. For instance, you may have an app that is supposedly free but has gimmicks inside, like "one tap buy," "character upgrade," or "send a rose" that takes your money!

Before you checkout, think: Am I buying this because I truly want it or just to get likes and attention?

Let's take control of our cash and spend mindfully on what matters most to us, not what society and social media push. I'll be real with you here; it can be hard work. But you've got this, and reading this chapter is the first step!

WHAT INFLUENCES SPENDING?

"Ooh, shiny!" My best friend Eliza exclaimed, grabbing the new smartphone model glistening under the spotlight. We were at our favorite mall, killing time before a movie, when the sleek device caught her eye. The pulsing store atmosphere instantly made me crave owning the glossy gadget too, though an hour earlier, I couldn't have cared less about upgrading.

I smiled, remembering the unit we learned in Psych class about how retailers engineer environments to tap into subconscious triggers to compelling purchases. Stores pump "new electronics" scent, blast Top 40 hits, and even spotlight impulse buys to exploit mental vulnerabilities.

Outside, I recounted more evidence of covert consumer influence from class. We left, making a pact to always question our purchasing decisions whenever the desire or impulse arose, rather than mindlessly following "everybody's doing it" scripts. Game recognizes game, and understanding the playbook made us savvier shoppers henceforth.

There are even more ways we are influenced to give out our hard-earned money:

Social Media Triggers Spending

Platforms use sneaky tactics, so you feel pressured to buy more stuff to get likes and followers. Ever seen someone post a perfect selfie holding a fancy Starbucks drink or unboxing some crazy expensive shoes? Now you suddenly feel like you "need" those things too.

Remember agonizing for weeks last year over buying those limited edition sneakers after your favorite influencer wouldn't stop flaunting them? Or how TikTok videos suddenly make you crave ordering delivery from viral food spots across town? Platforms know how to spark obsessive fear of missing out (FOMO).

Peers Strongly Steer Brand Choices

Raise your hand again if you've begged parents for the same brands as friends. Maybe it was LuluLemon outfits to match other cheerleaders. Or feeling forced only to wear sneaker brands considered cool this year.

Retail analysts trace items gaining traction first within "high-status" friend groups and school subcultures. Marketers instantly notice those trends on social media and then amplify the hype through wider influencer networks. Soon, no one will question why certain logos signal status and must-have identity symbols.

The takeaway? It's all orchestrated by companies benefiting when we pressure friends to wear their brands. Seeking validation through purchases rather than self-confidence and individuality lets marketers manipulate us.

Predictive Modeling Amplifies Trends

Feel like your phone spies on conversations? One girl mentioned struggling with acne to a friend. Despite never searching for skin care online, acne treatment ads suddenly flooded her Instagram feed. Another guy who posted about stress over college loans got bombarded with debt consolidation promotions.

Brands pay big money for machine learning algorithms, identifying consumer sentiment shifts faster than we realize them. Once signals emerge, market researchers instantly turn up targeted advertising to manipulate emotions. They benefit most from us feeling insecure or anxious enough to overspend on solutions.

The healthy takeaway? Next time ads seem psychically timed when you're vulnerable, realize that experts are "watching" what is happening and that that's the prime time to pause on big purchases. Don't let artificial intelligence trick you by capitalizing on temporary feelings or doubts about yourself!

Financial Illiteracy Enables Overspending

Most schools still don't teach key skills about managing income, creating budgets, and responsibly handling finances that unlock with adulthood. Gaps in financial literacy make it easier for all the other influences to sway your spending habits.

For example, 56% of Americans regret opening their first credit card with outrageously high 20%+ interest rates buried in fine print (Schulz, 2020). Fifty-four percent of American students feel wholly unprepared to compare student loan options (Reinicke, 2022). Most teens stumble blindly into costly financial mistakes that hurt them for years simply because no one warned them beforehand in any school curriculum.

The positive takeaway? Even though gaps in money management literacy exist, you're already getting way ahead of most people by reading this book! Let's learn from others' mistakes. Together, we can demand change while also taking responsibility through helpful tools like the chapters in this book, providing critical lifetime skills never formally taught to you before!

THREE WAYS SOCIAL MEDIA ENABLES BAD SPENDING HABITS

Social platforms claim they connect you to the world, but harmful spending triggers get buried behind cute filters and memes. Let's expose 3 prevalent ways social media unconsciously promotes financial wreckage:

Mythic lifestyles seem attainable: Ever wonder how influencers afford first-class worldwide travel and wardrobes full of designer brands? Social media portrays lavish lifestyles as affordable if you just use certain credit cards, financing plans, or brand deals. What doesn't get shown? Crippling interest charges and family money fueling "attainable" fairy tales.

Content glorifies reckless consumption: Scroll through popular content, and you'll notice much of the bite-sized entertainment implicitly normalizes excessive spending. Unboxing videos, clothing haul try-ons, product pushers–it's nonstop activation to buy more stuff. And don't get us started on luxury flaunts, posing with champagne and mansions bigger than your school.

Risky advice spreads unchecked: Unfortunately, misguided money tips also spread widely through copied posts and viral chatter. From exploiting financial aid loopholes to signing up for predatory quick cash schemes, social platforms allow questionable guidance to circulate without guardrails on credibility or fact-checking sources.

While convenience and connection abound online, we must remain vigilant against ideas subtly hurting our financial futures. Awareness is power! If it sounds way too good to be true, it probably is.

BUILDING HEALTHIER SPENDING HABITS

We've all mindlessly clicked "buy" and then regretted it later. Good news—you can transform into an intentional spender with consistent practice.

Bad habits only keep recurring due to short-term mood boosts. But retraining your brain to pause and check big purchases against priorities can reshape those destructive impulses.

Take late-night food delivery buys, for example; the apps ignite cravings with enticing deals precisely when willpower wanes. But that comfort snack doesn't satisfy deeper emotional voids. Identifying and attentively filling those needs correctly will curb the desire to order impulsively.

Combat over-consumption hijacked by outside pressures. Start building financial and mental peace by mindfully meeting needs, not endlessly chasing superficial fulfillment. You deserve to nurture inner wholeness. This info helps you begin that self-care journey toward intentional spending on your own terms!

If you find yourself overspending in certain categories like food delivery, clothing, or entertainment, invest time in journaling to uncover the root psychological drivers. Ask yourself thoughtful questions like:

- Why do I compulsively order in late at night when I'm not even hungry? Am I using food to de-stress or fill an emotional void?
- What need do all these new clothes serve? Am I trying to project a certain self-image or get validation by buying hot trends?
- Do I spend on events with friends to avoid missing out or loneliness? Would more meaningful social connections reduce this pressure?

Once you identify the emotional trigger tied to your wallet, you can problem-solve ways to healthily meet that need instead, whether through self-care, social support, or lifestyle changes. By addressing the root cause, changing harmful spending patterns becomes more sustainable in the long term. You don't have to do this alone. Seek counsel from your parents or a trusted adult if you're having trouble figuring things out.

WHAT IS A HABIT?

Essentially, habits are behaviors done automatically without thinking due to triggers. At first, forming a habit takes effort. But repeating an action in response to cues like locations, emotions, or times of day wires it into your brain's circuitry until it sticks. For example:

- checking Instagram sales every morning

- buying cookies when sad
- grabbing a latte before class every day

Habits form through a three-step loop—the cue, the routine behavior, and the rewarding feeling afterward.

Here's how it works:

1. **The Cue:** This is the trigger prompting a habitual behavior. Cues can be locations, emotional states, other people, preceding actions, time of day, or situations.
2. **The Routine:** This is the actual habitual behavior that plays out automatically as a response to the cue. This could be physical actions, mental projections, or emotional responses.
3. **The Reward:** A neurochemical rush provides temporary pleasure, relief, or escapism, wiring your brain to associate and anticipate this good feeling with your habit loop.

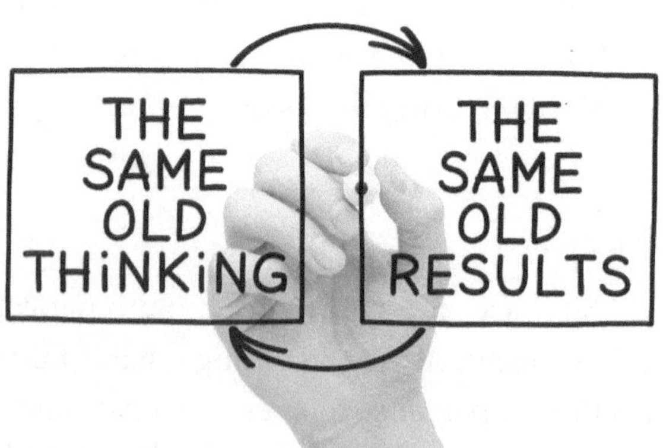

Image with permission of Piscine on iStock

These show how behaviors can become habits when rewards get anticipated. Seeing vending machines sparks cravings for sugar.

The cue is walking past them, the habit is purchasing candy bars, and the reward is temporarily satiating sweet cravings.

Over time, the cues automatically pull people into habit loops, even without them thinking about it. That's why they feel it is challenging to break at first. That's why it's crucial that we identify the cues and address their corresponding habits, which result in reckless spending or have other bad consequences. Remember our money mindset?

HOW DO SPENDING HABITS FORM?

Spending habits start small by repeating cues, actions, and reward loops until they feel automatic. For example, walking past candy in checkout lines repeatedly sparks sugar cravings. Giving in and purchasing chocolate bars leads to an energy boost.

Over time, merely seeing candy activates anticipatory neuro-chemical messaging, kicking off cravings before you even consciously register the sensation. Your brain learns to associate and then expects to feel better after yielding to the impulse buy, prompting habitual spending.

Why is it Hard to Break Spending Habits?

Disrupting existing habit circuits requires extra mental effort to avoid familiar patterns, which feels innately taxing. Additionally, changes initially eliminate anticipated feel-good neurochemicals your brain relies on, causing temporary discomfort when first substituting with healthier rewards.

This dual difficulty causes many people to default back to their counterproductive habits. Good spending habits become the default by enduring the discomfort period of forming new triggers and rewards. Always strive for long-term satisfaction, not the temporary highs that leave as quickly as they came!

How Knowing the "Why" Helps Change Habits

Self-awareness around the emotional or social void you aim to fill through specific purchases allows you to substitute bad habits with healthier habits and truly fulfill your core needs. If retail therapy distracts from loneliness, deeper social bonds can provide genuine connection without financial strain.

Changing habits is no "walk in the park," So If you're having difficulty figuring out this void, it can help to have these conversations with a parent, trusted friend, or therapist.

What Impacts Social Spending Habits

Many overlapping forces shape youth financial behaviors, including:

Teachers and role models: Early money lessons we're taught, or not taught, influence attitudes we carry into adulthood. Having savvy mentors who model smart savings and intentional spending provides a road map to follow.

Media and entertainment: Pop culture impacts aspirations and normalizes materialism, like celebrities flaunting opulent lifestyles. However, content creators teaching financial literacy provide healthier blueprints.

Cultural values and religion: Some faiths encourage moderated spending through principles like tithing or conserving. Cultural values prize frugality and prudence, ingraining habits, and eschewing over-consumption.

In reality, ongoing dynamic interactions between these factors and others unique to each person's journey impact the development of financial behaviors. But with self-awareness and helpful mentors, we can choose who and what influences us.

Now, you know how your spending can influence your environment and the people around you. The chapter doesn't end yet. I'm sharing with you my secret tricks and tips, which I used to keep my bad spending habits in check. You can follow them too!

TIPS AND TRICKS TO SPEND LESS

Watch any epic hero's tale, which started small—Harry Potter receiving his first Hogwarts letter or Superman helping his parents on their farm. Great journeys begin modestly before rising. Let's channel our inner wizard as we walk through 15 practical, bite-sized saving tips categorized by expense area and a short example scenario for each.

Entertainment and recreation:

- Borrow books/games from the library instead of buying: Save $15-20 monthly by buying new young adult fiction.
- Use free streaming trial periods, then cancel: Set 1 month of ad-free music, then revert back to free. Beware of paid auto-subscribes!
- Attend free community events: Enjoy outdoor concerts rather than paying for arena shows.

Clothing and accessories:

- Shop end-of-season sales for big discounts: For example, buy holiday dresses at 70% off post-New Year.
- Swap gently used items with friends: Freshen wardrobe trading last season's tops.

- Learn basic mending/alterations: Repair ripped jeans rather than replacing them.

Technology upgrades:

- Sell used device before upgrading to offset cost: Recover ~50% smartphone value financing next one.
- Use refurbished electronic options: Purchase affordable off-lease laptops directly from manufacturers.
- Unlock phone capabilities yourself: Enable built-in hotspot 5G data, saving $15/month carrier fees.

Food and dining:

- Limit eating out to twice weekly: For example, drop takeout frequency from four times to biweekly.
- Brown bag lunch thrice a week: Pack sandwiches/fruit rather than buying $10 meals out.
- Learn to meal prep efficiently: Spend Sunday cooking staples like rice, roasted vegetables and so on.

School and activities:

- Carpool with friends to events: Save money by alternating driving with your friends to events or splitting the gas cost.
- Rent formal wear instead of purchasing: Before you pay for that $100 dress, is there an option to borrow it? If so, borrow it to minimize costs. It's only for an event anyway.
- Take advantage of free student software: Downloading Windows/Microsoft Office education bundles could save you $100s.

DO YOU NEED IT OR WANT IT?

Sixteen-year-old Alex stared wide-eyed at their first-ever paycheck, hands shaking with excitement. The $463.18 unlocked endless spending possibilities—sweet sneakers, the latest iPhone, and wild nights out with friends.

Alex's parents chuckled, equally excited about this financial milestone.

"Before you start spending every which way, let your old folks teach you something," Dad said. He explained the importance of distinguishing between needs and wants when managing money.

Needs are life's essential expenses—food, shelter, transportation. Needs are critical for basic functioning. Wants are non-essentials, however enjoyable—trendy gadgets, entertainment, luxury goods.

Alex pictured the flashy items on their wish list, grasping how few qualified as true necessities. Still, balance seemed possible. By prioritizing needs first, they could moderately indulge wants and achieve longer-term money goals.

Clearly, distinguishing between needs and wants is critical when aligning spending with income, savings, and financial priorities. Consciously identifying expenses in those categories allows for thoughtful money management.

By consciously identifying expenses in those categories, we can thoughtfully align spending with income, savings goals, and financial priorities.

CAN YOU IDENTIFY YOUR NEEDS VERSUS YOUR WANTS?

As a teenager, it can be hard to know the difference between things you need to spend money on and those extra wants that seem so appealing. However, prioritizing needs over impulse buys is critical for saving money.

Let's try a month-long spending tracking challenge together. I'll provide a simple template to write down every purchase you make, big or small. At the end of each day, categorize each expense as either a "Need"—something essential for your daily life/survival, or a "Want"—an optional extra.

Date	Expense description	Amount	Category

As the month passes, log every expense you make, no matter how small. Reflect on each purchase; did you spend out of necessity or desire? Label it "Need" or "Want" accordingly.

Some reflection questions on ambiguous purchases:

- How severely would skipping this purchase impact my daily functioning?
- Did I buy this more out of desire or essential need?

When you feel tempted to buy something impulsively:

- If in a store, wait 24 hours before deciding. Revisit whether you still want or need the item a day later with a fresh perspective.
- Online, add appealing items to your wish list or cart, then log out. Check back the next day—did your interest remain or lose its initial shine? Did you even remember to check?

Giving into spontaneous cravings versus intentional needs is a key distinction. If the initial excitement fades after a short wait, you likely didn't truly need the item.

PUTTING IT ALL TOGETHER: BUILDING A SPENDING PLAN

Earlier, we discussed different types of budgeting approaches—percentage-based, zero-sum, and reverse budgets. Now that you've tracked your spending and assessed needs versus wants, it's time to re-evaluate your personalized spending plan to ensure it aligns with your financial priorities.

Step 1: Track Your Spending

Open your favorite money app from the previous chapters, or grab a notebook. Time to log every dollar spent over the next week! Document it all, whether it's iced oat milk lattes, band merch, or Uber Eats. This builds awareness of current habits before making changes. I'll demonstrate with my daily Starbucks run... input *"$5.50 Caramel Macchiato" into the app.*

Step 2: Categorize Expenses

Sort your purchases into Needs or Wants buckets, as I've shown you in the earlier section. Remember, be honest about this. Don't forget items like housing, food, and transport go into Needs. Entertainment and shopping land under Wants. Again, it all depends on you and what you really need versus what you want. Unsure about something? Ask yourself, "Could I survive without this?"

Tip: Some expenses may only partially qualify as Needs!

For example, I could brew coffee at home instead of hitting Starbucks daily. So I'll put half that amount under needs and the rest as wants. I will also make a note in my budget that I should try making this at home or skipping it for a few days and see if that is a change to my budget that I like.

Step 3: Set Savings Goals

What are your big money dreams? Whether starting a business, retiring early, conquering college debt-free, or having debt-free vacation plans, define 1-3 specific savings targets. This focuses on spending reductions on stuff that matters to you rather than abstract "budgeting." For me, escaping student loans and bonding with nature are huge goals.

Step 4: Create Your Plan

Now, compare your total monthly expenses with your total income. Craft an organized blueprint balancing monthly income versus expenses in aligned categories, with a surplus going toward your savings goals.

Step 5: Stick With It!

Follow your plan, tweaking amounts as life changes occur. Like anything worth doing, maintaining good financial behaviors takes practice, but determination pays off hugely over time! Ready to cement healthy money habits and live your dreams? Then step up and dominate your financial destiny!

LEVEL UP YOUR FINANCIAL GAME

We've covered vital ground in this chapter about taking control of spending—life's most fundamental money skill!

First, assessing influences to reveal where external pressures steer us astray from our priorities is crucial. Then, differentiating fleeting wants from ongoing needs will inform smarter allocation aligned with values. Finally, creating customized spending blueprints enables both mindful consumption and targeted savings

With a fresh understanding of how intentional planning tames our impulses, harnessing behavioral cues and bridges—we are presented with trade-offs to fund future dreams. Your financial foundation is now set! Consistent tracking is key, but know plans and adapt as life shifts occur.

Now equipped with strong money management basics, we're ready to boost financial firepower! Let's master banking tools, from accounts to taxes, that amplify returns through savvy saving and investing vehicles.

I'll break down key options in bite-sized bits—no intimidating jargon, I promise! With strategies catered to teens, we'll elevate your wealth-creation toolkit. Think you've got what it takes? Then let's level up and conquer the next chapter together — Onward!

CHAPTER FIVE

CONQUERING BANKING

Relying solely on cash means no paper trail for your transactions. That means no record of income, expenses, and savings. These records are actually crucial for building financial credibility. Without them, you cannot pursue loans for purchases like cars or homes down the road. Why? Because lenders use your financial records to weigh how well you handle money.

Most teenagers still have a lot to learn about utilizing banking services efficiently. But have no fear!

In this chapter, we will explore all you need to know about the role banks play in the economy, the array of services they offer, how to choose your ideal bank, and how digital banking tools can equip tech-savvy teens like you with more control over your finances than ever before!

By the end, you'll feel confident and eager to leverage banks to grow your money securely rather than store it under your mattress. Let's get conquering!

KNOWING YOUR BANK

Banks let you securely store your money while earning interest on savings accounts. You've seen the cool plastic cards in your parents' wallets, right? Those are either credit cards or debit cards, which enable easy online purchases without carrying envelopes of bills.

But those aren't the only perks that come with banking. Banks also:

- allow you to save money in secure accounts that grow through interest—bonus money added to your account—over time
- provide transaction records and statements that are helpful in keeping track of money and building financial credibility
- offer loans that you could use for big purchases like your first car, home, or even a business

Banks provide companies loans for expenses like equipment. These loans charge interest—extra money paid over time.

Responsible borrowers use loans strategically and then repay on schedule. You can benefit from interest, too! By storing cash in teen savings accounts, your money grows over time while sitting there.

However, handling money carries significant responsibility. Banks face strict government supervision through agencies like the *Federal Deposit Insurance Corporation* (FDIC). The FDIC monitors operations to ensure banks keep enough reserve cash and make fair lending decisions—not shady ones.

These FDIC regulations help you feel secure in storing your hard-earned cash. You want your savings handled responsibly by your bank, not used irresponsibly like money at a wild party! Note that the FDIC can only guarantee the safety of your money up to $250,000. That's why you should verify that the bank, especially online banks, you intend to save with is backed by the FDIC.

Staying informed on banking basics means leveraging banks wisely as you save for big future purchases. Let your money work for you!

TYPES OF BANKS

Get ready for a crash course in banking flavors! Just like ice cream, banks come in lots of varieties. But instead of chocolate or rocky roads, we've got central, commercial, and public sectors and more banks. Each type specializes in different money management services for governments, businesses, and everyday folks like you and me. Let's explore so you can decide which financial institution suits your needs as your stash of cash grows bigger!

Central Banks

Central banks establish monetary policies and ensure bank systems are stable worldwide and in individual countries. You won't open an account here as an individual. But you benefit from initiatives introduced by the *United States Federal Reserve* to stimulate healthy savings interest rates and regulate inflation levels so the dollars you earn don't lose value over time. Central banks are the money custodians of entire nations!

Commercial Banks

Now, commercial banks like *Chase, Citibank*, and *Wells Fargo* cater directly to us regular folk. These drive most day-to-day banking with branches you see in local neighborhoods and cities. They provide convenient access to physical locations for in-person support, *Automated Teller Machines* (ATMs) to withdraw cash anytime, and functional mobile apps to check balances on the go.

Commercial banks offer various services and account types, such as *checking* and *savings accounts* best suited for everyday usage. Commercial banks also provide special accounts, like the *certificates of deposit* (CDs), and fixed-term deposit accounts. This means that you deposit your money for a given period and receive interest until what's called the *maturity date*. It's just another name for the expiry date. Unlike a savings account, the interest rates on CDs are supercharged!

Another vital service commercial banks offer is the consumer lending system, which includes credit cards or personal loans. This is not for you to worry about now.

Savings and Loan Associations/Thrifts

If the phrase "savings and loan" sounds familiar, your parents or grandparents may have banked at one of these institutions in the past. Before commercial banks offered robust savings interest rates, Savings and Loans specialized in savings accounts and mortgage lending as their primary offerings. Many of these were acquired by big banks, but some still exist, like *Savings Institute Bank and Trust Company*.

Investment Banks

Ever seen movies with Wall Street bigwigs running around trading stocks and arranging massive company mergers? Well, that's the lucrative domain of investment banks like *Goldman Sachs* and *JP Morgan*. They assist high-net-worth corporations, entrepreneurs, and governments with activities like raising investment capital, mergers and acquisitions, restructuring, and more complex financial undertakings that typical commercial banks don't handle.

Online/Direct Banks

Lastly, with the 21st-century rise of digital services, innovative "online-only" banks popped up like *Chime, Ally Bank*, and *Charles Schwab Bank*. Without the overhead costs of physical branches, they offer flexible apps for convenient access along with debit cards, checking accounts with decent interest, automated savings plans, and investment platforms. These are great options for tech-savvy teens who just need basic mobile banking and don't care about seeing tellers in person.

KNOW THE BANK'S SUPERPOWERS

Now that you know the different types of banks, let's check out the excellent services they offer to make handling money easier for busy teens like you! Banks provide helpful tools for safely storing cash, growing savings, paying friends back for stuff, and financing big future purchases as an adult. Here are the primary services offered:

Accepting deposits: Banks store customers' cash securely in accounts while providing convenient access to those funds via branches, ATMs, online portals, and mobile apps.

ATM services: Banks connect user-friendly ATM kiosks to customer accounts for self-service cash withdrawals, balance checks, and other essential transactions, often for a small fee.

Loans: Banks provide financing for major expenses by lending qualified borrowers money upfront that gets repaid over time plus interest charges.

Bank guarantee: Banks vow to cover losses for business customers if their clients can't pay vendors, which is useful for reassuring sellers when buyers lack credit history.

Check/cheque payment: Checks allow account holders to securely pay others directly from bank funds by providing a written order to make specific withdrawals against the payer's account balance.

Collection and payment of credit instruments: Banks handle the monthly consolidation, billing, and collection of loan payments, credit card balances, and debts owed by borrowers and credit account holders.

Overdraft features: Overdrafts allow customers to exceed their account balance for purchases, essentially providing short-term financing that gets repaid with interest fees.

Consultancy: Bank consultants offer advisory services, guiding customers on best practices, regulations, digital capabilities, retirement planning, and other financial matters.

Credit cards: Banks issue branded credit cards, enabling responsible customers to purchase now and repay sums owed later.

Debit cards: Banks instantly provide branded debit card deduction purchases from customer accounts instead of allowing repayment over time like credit cards.

Foreign currency exchange: Banks can securely convert currencies across borders, enabling customers to access foreign goods, services, or funds seamlessly.

Online banking: Internet banking portals allow 24/7 account access for monitoring balances, making peer payments, depositing checks, updating details, and conducting other transactions digitally.

Mobile banking: Mobile banking apps provide digital account access and transaction capabilities via internet-connected smartphones and devices.

PRO GUIDE TO CHOOSING A BANK

If you were a superhero, think of the bank as a weapon. You must choose them carefully. The problem is that there are a ton out there, and we often don't know which to choose and rely on! Believe me, I faced analysis paralysis, too, when I first compared options.

You've got combustible credit unions, online disruptors like *Chime* shaking things up, not to mention titans like *Chase* blanketing the airwaves! All of them compete for your coins by touting reasons why they're best.

But here's the secret—no one-size-fits-all "right choice" exists. Only what resonates most with your lifestyle, priorities, and beliefs. The perfect bank for me, living large in Los Angeles and lugging my camera gear to shoot, likely looks totally different from an ideal match for a high schooler in Houston saving up for a scooter!

After applying my time-tested formula to cut through the noise, you'll become a savvy bank account owner. Think of this like deciding which aesthetic filter best showcases your vibe. Or choose that go-to Spotify playlist to capture your soul!

Here's a step-by-step guide to filtering options and identifying your personalized financial BFF...

Step 1: Catalog your must-have capabilities like mobile check deposit and fee-free overdraft versus nice-to-have features like snazzy debit card designs, and so on.

For example, I prioritized a mobile banking app enabling quick peer-to-peer payments to friends given frequent concert ticket splits. Meanwhile, I couldn't care less about branch proximity since I live online. List your core functional needs first before considering flashy extras.

Step 2: Crossmatch required features against the bank offering list, filtering out ones missing key pillars.

I ruled out smaller regional banks and online only neobanks lacking robust phone customer service since I wanted live human access as a backup. If you must have a widely available local ATM network, cross off digital-first options.

Step 3: Shortlist 2-3 closest matches and validate through family/friends as current users.

My saxophonist buddy Charlie banks with Chase and gave me the insider scoop on their account perks and pitfalls to guide my shortlist. See if your parents or teammates have informed opinions to leverage.

Step 4: Schedule Test Banking Days meeting with finalists to get a feel for real-life experience.

I sat down with branch reps from my top two choices to articulate my needs as a teen and ask all the nitty-gritty questions about overdraft rules and fund transfer latency expectations.

Step 5: Trust your gut in the final selection, focusing less on rewards hype and more on alignment.

Between big brand Chase and smaller First Republic, the latter felt less impersonal and better matched my maturing financial literacy needs. I followed my intuition.

Below is a table that demonstrates the above steps:

Feature	Bank A	Bank B	Bank C	Bank D	Bank E
No monthly fees	No	Yes	Yes	No	Yes
Mobile check deposit	Yes	Yes	Yes	Yes	No
Interest rate ≥ 1%	No	Yes	Yes	Yes	No
Established > 10 years	Yes	No	Yes	No	Yes
Good mobile app rating	Yes	Yes	No	Yes	Yes

Evaluation: With more options on the table, we can see Banks B and C firmly match top priorities around no monthly fees and solid interest rates. Bank C's longer history counters B's app maturity. Bank D also pays competitive interest, but its monthly costs rule it out. Since mobile experience, longevity, and low costs are all met by either B or C, the ultimate selection depends on your preference.

OPENING A BANK ACCOUNT

Alright, money mavens, we've assessed the key traits separating banking critical selection criteria. Now it's time for the big reveal... *cue drumroll...* let's walk through opening your first account and turning calculator-eyed bank bots into loyal cash compadres!

1. Shortlist the top 2-3 bank partners:

- Log the key attributes like minimum balances, interest rates, and overdraft policy in the spreadsheet for easy comparison, as shown above.
- Have your parents help you qualify choices based on their own user experiences to identify potential pitfalls.

2. Schedule intro calls:

- For online-only banks, ask about historical security breach statistics, fraud prevention measures, and redundancy assurances. Redundancy assurances refer to backup systems and protections allowing bank operations to continue functioning securely even if specific technology components are disrupted.
- For traditional banks, prepare questions about account transition support when leaving for college.
- Inquire about the full fee schedule associated with teen checking and savings accounts, and ask what requirements or actions can be taken to waive specific fees.

3. Conduct final evaluation:

- Schedule a visit to the bank or contact the bank through live chat via their websites. Some banks offer video chat, too. During the video chat walk-through, have representatives demonstrate mobile check deposit, peer-to-peer payment, and budget tracking features in-app to confirm usability and intuitiveness.
- Validate any benefit claims by researching current customer sentiment on third-party review sites.

4. Review account terms thoroughly:

- Carefully inspect fine print sections detailing fee schedules to ensure no surprise costs.
- Confirm that the interest rates on savings accounts match the advertised annual percentage yield (APY) or the annual interest rates of the accounts.

5. Digitally submit an account application:

- For traditional banks like *Chase* or *Wells* requiring in-branch paperwork, set up appointments to finalize signatures.

6. Fund account with an initial deposit:

- Document the minimum balance requirements during the signup phase and prepare a transfer or deposit to meet them if necessary.

7. Complete identity verification:

- Have government ID card, social security info, and mobile device available to complete multi-factor authentication intrinsic to all bank onboarding flows.
- Setup account passwords with maximum entropy best practices.

8. Download the native mobile application:

- During the first sessions, poke around the interface and ensure features like biometric login, P2P payments, and debit activity controls are enabled.

- Toggle on SMS alerts for balance thresholds so no surprises occur.

9. Congrats and welcome communication:

- Carefully review onboarding material detailing available account capabilities and management practices.
- Log calendar reminder to set scheduled recurring transfers to savings in pursuit of automatic discipline.

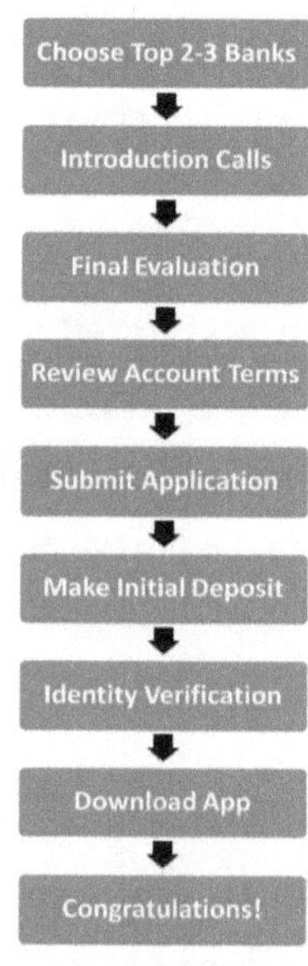

BANKING TIPS TO REMEMBER

Let's drop some insider banking expertise I've accrued over decades traversing tricky financial landscapes. Consider these battle-tested tips for dodging bank foot mines and shooting savings to soaring new heights!

Tip #1 - Check Your Bank App's Rating

Before opening any account, install their iPhone/Android app even as a non-customer to poke around. Pay attention to design, ease of finding features, and user reviews in the Store. You want mobile banking to be as smooth as Snapchat!

Tip #2 – Ask Friends About Experiences

Doing recon on banks? Ask peers on social media for candid feedback if they're already customers. Get the real scoop about annoying fees and bad app glitches your pals encountered firsthand with Chase, Wells, and others.

Tip #3 – Have Multiple Savings Spots

Once income and cash gifts pick up, consider dividing money between two trusted banks instead of one. Protects better against system hacks or hardware failure losing everything.

Tip #4-Evaluate All Reward Perks, Not Just Points

Opening the first credit card soon? Don't just compare airline miles and signup bonuses. Check whether other perks like cell phone insurance, fee credits, and lounge access waivers are included even on student cards before applying.

Tip #5 – Watch Bank Video Reviews on YouTube

Financial creators on YouTube post really thorough step-by-step account walk-throughs about the pros, cons, and hidden gotchas. Search "[Bank Name] Review 2022/2023" and filter by most recent. Study before committing to avoid surprise pitfalls!

Tip #6 – Ask What Happens if You Must Close the Account

If something big forces closing a new account fast, like identity theft or nasty fees, know policies upfront around credit score impact or rejoining that bank later to avoid issues when crisis strikes.

Tip #7 – Read all Notifications from Your Bank App

When downloading your bank's phone app, enable push alerts—transaction notices, balance info, etc. This helps catch suspicious stuff fast! Review all alerts ASAP in case of account takeover attempts requiring urgent response!

Tip #8 – Discuss New Financial Products After Getting Started

Already got help opening your first checking account? Circle back for later chats about budgeting tools, auto-saving, and investing options to upgrade money skills over time.

Tip #9 – Ask Friends About Their Favorite Budgeting App Features

Request app demos from money-savvy pals showing their favorite tools for tracking allowance inflows/outflows and saving/spending goals. Test the same features in your new banking app!

Tip #10 - Always Type Bank URLs Manually

When linking accounts, never click slick login links. Manually navigate to known bank URLs every time. This prevents scammers from stealing your login info via *phishing*. Stay secure as the money starts piling up!

BANKING IN THE DIGITAL AGE

You may fondly remember accompanying parents inside bank office space and layouts containing neat rows of seasoned tellers and smartly dressed managers. These traditional banks formed the financial backbones of communities everywhere for decades.

The winds of change now whistle through what were once long-standing bank pillars of the industry. Slick digital disruptors have arisen, plugged into the 24/7 connected world. They tempt the next generations with promises of seamlessness, self-service, and savings.

To understand this shift, we first need to examine how traditional and new digital banks differ. I'll overview how traditional and modern banking formats compare key factors teenagers focus on, like accessibility, functionality, safety, and pricing.

Also, the knowledge can help facilitate more informed family discussions around banking and finance.

Once you see the pros and cons of each option, you can decide what works best for you. Should you stick with old-fashioned banks or go digital? Maybe a bit of both?

TRADITIONAL BANKING

For the past 100+ years, big traditional banks like *Chase*, *Wells Fargo*, and *Bank of America* have built many branch locations in local neighborhoods to serve surrounding communities. This lets customers meet in person with staff for help opening accounts, making deposits/withdrawals, getting loans, and more during weekday business hours.

The face-to-face service and paper signature approach provide confidence for older generations. But locations closing at 5-6 p.m. sharp cause headaches for busy high schoolers! Traditional banks also lag a bit in upgrading online and phone support to match the 24/7 convenience offered by trendy fintech startups.

MODERN DIGITAL BANKING

Unlike big banks, new financial technology startups recognize most young people's lives happen online. In response, mobile banks like Chime, Current, and Aspiration built user-friendly apps and websites focused on self-service without physical branches.

Without costly localized buildings to pay for, many digital players skip irritating maintenance fees and minimum balances that limit savings growth for traditional accounts. Instead, they lure customers through convenience—opening accounts and getting loans entirely through laptops and iPhones backed by automation.

Savvy, experienced designers also build financial literacy into offerings. Examples include customizable savings rules, spending summaries by category, and guides to wisely use stuff like credit cards earlier to build good histories.

Of course, digital banking still has some trade-offs. Fraud remains a threat without in-person identity checks. Also, the convenience can tempt users to withdraw more than they should. But with the money mindset and skill you've gained by reading this book, you won't fall for this!

That said, many traditional banks now offer both robust mobile apps and local branches. This gives customers both digital convenience and ongoing access to human bankers when needed.

HOW THEY COMPARE

Traditional and online banks have some big differences in how they operate, even if they share similar goals around managing money and teaching financial skills. These differences lead to real pros and cons to think about when picking your ideal bank. The table below highlights some of the key trade-offs between the two models:

Dimension	Traditional banks	Online banks
Accessibility	Localized branches for personalized service needs during workweek business hours	Online + app availability 24/7
Core Features	Standard savings/checking accounts	Budgeting and auto-save tools are built-in to monitor transactions and effortlessly accumulate wealth
Security	In-person identity verification and paperwork exchange promote trust	Multi-factor and biometric authentication ensure security without needing to visit the bank
Cost Considerations	Some banks charge fees to operate an account with them	No minimum balance requirements and subscription models increase affordability

As the summary shows, while big traditional banks benefit from established reputations and in-person guidance, their physical branch reliance causes struggles in shifting to digital services compared to mobile-first rivals. At the same time, streamlined digital experiences lack personalized human touchpoints beyond bot FAQs.

In the end, consumers choose based on preferences around convenience, customization, safety, and value. Prioritize what matters most to you and pick what aligns with your life stage and needs. Maybe try out both before choosing the one that suits you best. There's no harm in trying!

EMBRACING DIGITAL BANKING

As a member of Gen Z or Alpha, you are immersed in digital services impacting nearly all aspects of your life, including managing personal finances.

From utilizing peer-to-peer (P2P) payment apps like PayPal, Venmo, or CashApp to pay friends, to leveraging mobile banking apps offered by traditional institutions, you likely conduct financial activities across an expanding ecosystem of digital banking technologies.

Even purchasing items in brick-and-mortar stores has shifted toward contactless payments with services like Apple Pay and Google Pay integrated into your smartphone devices.

As these diverse financial management tools and apps connect, they have effectively created a digital banking "superhub" capable of handling your day-to-day banking activities without the traditional reliance on physical bank branches.

This presents an immense opportunity for you to adopt modern, convenient digital finance tools early on—cultivating smart money habits that will reap rewards well into adulthood. The sections ahead guide selecting and navigating preferred digital banking tools tailored to leveraging technology as a Gen Z consumer.

Traditional Banking vs. New Digital Offerings

While industry juggernauts like *Chase, Bank of America,* and *Wells Fargo* trace their roots back over a century, they have evolved to offer digital banking features that mirror popular cash management apps from disruptive fintech startups. Their mobile offerings may lack certain innovations gaining traction among younger demographics like you.

Conversely, a bevy of new banking providers builds products explicitly with Gen Z tech behaviors in mind—whether standalone cash management apps or digital-first bank replacements. As you compare options, key questions include:

- Does the provider focus specifically on serving young consumers' needs?
- How sophisticated and easy-to-use is the mobile user experience?
- Are useful money tools like budgeting and financial advice included?
- Can accounts seamlessly integrate with other popular peer payment apps?

While traditional banks provide peace of mind and account security, they may fall short of connecting with youth preferences.

HOW TECH IS CHANGING BANKING

The wave of digital banking has brought huge positive changes in how young people can manage money on their phones, compared to only using old-school physical bank branches. Cool new features like flexible payments to friends and handy tools to automate saving unlock awesome possibilities. But this fast pace of change also makes parents hesitant to trust disruptive new financial systems immediately.

Benefits of App Payments

Digital payments allowing "bankless" peer-to-peer sending offer versatility in instantly moving money to friends without old limits. Young users love payment apps for quick things like:

- paying back a buddy for fronting you cash for pizza
- having allowance deposited right into a mobile banking app
- buying stuff online without needing physical debit cards

"Bankless" avoids hassles like carrying cards everywhere. Streamlined access introduces convenience.

Concerns Around New Systems

However, these bankless features also carry risks if not built safely —from accidental user errors to potential fraud hacking personal data or even crypto theft. Oversight rules around fast-changing fintech tools aren't as strong yet compared to traditional banking's 80+ years of standards. Important details in regulations remain unclear.

Without rock-solid FDIC protection that shields bank accounts, linking to risky apps could seriously threaten college funds if hacked. Adoption without enough guards in place does raise fair challenges. Being mindful and careful online can help keep your money safe. It's good to know that some online banks are also FDIC-backed, like *CreditKarma*.

Regulating Digital Payments

Governments are quickly building guardrails that allow awesome digital innovation and reduce big threats:

- stronger ID checks and account access hacker protections
- extending FDIC-level safety nets to more pre-approved providers

- clearer reporting standards around risks
- total visibility for users on how private data gets used

Top apps now even qualify outright as full "banks" after meeting strict new benchmarks—safer picks for integrating into young people's financial lives. Standards improve every year.

So, while money apps seem "wild west" now compared to classic banks, integrity pillars remain steady despite quick changes. Not reckless chaos, but responsible evolution unlocks amazing possibilities while respecting the old foundations parents know.

A Tough but Fulfilling Journey

In this chapter, we explored the transforming 21st-century personal banking landscape. We learned how traditional physical banks and emerging digital banking models compare across key categories like accessibility, features, security, and costs.

You now understand the unique services banks provide and the trade-offs between established titans and innovative fintech disruptors. We also covered how advancing technologies introduce conveniences but raise regulatory challenges.

Making the right choice isn't always easy. You can operate a hybrid banking system, and don't forget that you don't have to walk this journey alone. Seek advice from your parents to help guard your decision. They are the pioneers of the new-age banking, after all!

As we progress in our PRIME finance journey, we build critical foundations. Now that you understand banking dynamics, we'll focus on exploring early income sources and paying taxes to propel financial capability further.

The next chapter dives into the range of traditional and modern side hustles teens leverage to start earning and saving money, along with the ins and outs of tax. Yes, tax!

CHAPTER SIX

EARNING MONEY AND PAYING TAXES

Choose a job you love, and you will never have to work a day in your life.

— CONFUCIUS

My heart broke discovering a viral TikTok video of teen Imani sobbing after opening her first job paycheck. Through confused tears, she vents:

"I babysat 20 hours every week expecting $800 bucks! But my check was only $620? Where did $180 go? Did the government rob me?!"

I know exactly how devastating that first tax bite feels, ransacking income and shattering excitement. When I was 16 staring at my $510 check instead of the expected $600, almost 15% had vanished from my minimum wage restaurant job!

I desperately wished to hug Imani, provide comfort, and say I understand—it's brutal seeing taxes hijack what you worked for. But it does all make sense with time and learning.

You see, upon reflection, I know this universal growing pain actually presents a golden opportunity to illuminate why tax contributions matter... and how strategic planning around deductions can help young earners keep more income while modeling responsible citizenship.

So I want to tell Imani directly if she reads this:

Dry your tears, girl! With financial awareness comes power. I'm writing this book to explain why understanding taxes empowers our net income success. Consider me your big Gen Z sis, ready to educate and support you on optimizing earnings minus confusing deductions. Let's shed light on this together!

UNDERSTANDING INCOME

Money makes the world go round—but have you pondered exactly where your money might come from someday? Beyond whatever cash Mom and Dad provide now or summer job paychecks, many creative income sources await you! The first step toward tapping new income streams is comprehending how people earn money.

As we established when building budgets in Chapter 3, tracking income flow is crucial for financial control. Beyond balancing spending in the present, income also fuels our biggest dreams and long-term ambitions! The right earnings vehicle can transport us toward goals like college, apartments, or global adventures.

We all dream of picking a career path we feel passionate about. But first, what does "income" actually mean? Income *is money earned from various sources like jobs, investments, government benefits, or even gifts.*

As students, most of you have limited incomes today. Maybe you walk dogs, referee youth sports, or run errands for the elderly neighbor down the street. Perhaps you get a small weekly allowance for household chores like cleaning or yard work. Or if you're really industrious, you might operate a mini business mowing lawns or creating arts and crafts for cash.

How Income Impacts Life

Earning personal income reduces dependence on others for expenses. You gain control to save for goals aligned with your interests rather than negotiate with guardians. Income lets you afford wants without begging your parents.

More vitally, early earning builds real-world financial skills to generate greater career wealth later. Remember, income requires delivering value others pay you for.

Strategic earning allows properly steering your financial destiny over time, impacting lifestyle and achieving long-term visions. Teen savings through jobs can ultimately fund major milestones ahead, like college.

Bottom line—income enables financial freedom! Cravings become affordable passions minus parental pestering. Spread your wings and seize discretionary spending power!

Types of Income

Beyond traditional wages, many income options exist depending on your skills, interests, and life stage. Common ways to earn money include:

- **Salaries and Hourly Wages:** Compensation from providing services as an employee. For example, summer lifeguard salaries or restaurant tip income.
- **Interest/Investments:** Earnings from loaning, investing, or depositing saved capital. For instance, interest on savings accounts or investment portfolio dividends.
- **Business Ownership:** Profits derived from sales and services of owned businesses. For example, retail store revenue after expenses or influencer ad monetization.

I get it—not all income types are accessible yet as a teen. But countless hourly wage or summer jobs eagerly welcome young employees. Entrepreneurial business ventures can thrive early in the booming internet landscape with the right inspiration.

Here is a list of 15 teen-friendly jobs within the U.S. with their average hourly pay and required skills:

Job Title	Hourly Pay	Skills Needed
Babysitter	$16.73	Childcare, trustworthiness, activity planning
Pet sitter	$14.76	Animal handling, home access responsibility
Lawnmower	$15.73	Outdoor labor, lawn care equipment operation
Dog walker	$14.10	Animal experience, neighborhood familiarity
Camp counselor	$12.67	Outdoor activity facilitation, risk management, teamwork
Youth coach	$15.17	Sports knowledge, leadership, maturity
Tutor	$16.94	Academic mastery, teaching ability, patience
Lifeguard	$15.37	CPR certification, swimming ability, vigilance
Receptionist	$12.01	Organization, phone manners, computer literacy
Restaurant server	$9.83 + tips	Customer service, food/drink awareness, stamina
Retail sales	$11.37	Product knowledge, organization, orderly displays
Web design	$16.61	Coding skills, creative visuals, SEO instincts
Referee	$9.88	Sporting Rules literacy, decision confidence, fitness
Trash collector	$15.34	Heavy lifting ability, early hours on feet, safety focus
Car washer	$9.91	Auto cleaning expertise, marketing hustle

Note that these figures vary and depend on several factors, like your state, the size of the company, and so on.

FIRST JOBS & CAREER EXPLORATION

Congrats on coming this far; it likely means you're daydreaming about freedom and extra cash from an inaugural job hunt! Well, buckle up, because reading this section gives you an edge in the job market and puts you a mile ahead in securing that ideal job that offers more than just a paycheck. You see, a job builds *long-term skills,* too! Let's uncover the first jobs preparing you for adult career success.

An Overview of Common Job Types

Four primary categories exist for starter positions while navigating school or other obligations:

Full-Time (30+ hrs/week): The employee salary and dedicated schedule resemble that of adult jobs, but expect trade-offs that provide room to balance workload with academics and socializing. For example, retail, childcare, and office admin roles commonly offer full-time teen hours.

Part-Time: This might be the ideal work-life balance for students! Reduced weekly hours—under 30—allow you to take on job responsibilities and other commitments. Look at roles like tutors, referees, and golf caddies.

Seasonal: Summer camp counselors, resort staffers, spring landscapers, holiday brand associates, and more leverage your availability into short-term focused work.

Temporary: Temporary jobs provide project or event-based work, unlike permanent roles. Consider catering waiters, registration assistants, or data entry gigs for temporary jobs. Once the task is done, the job ends, and you move to the next.

10 Tips for Searching First Jobs

We know selecting that first job is important for future success, not just short-term paper chasing. You want to build legit skills that flex career muscles for the long haul while also collecting checks and connecting with awesome co-workers. No doubt! Here are some valuable tips that will help ease your search for a first job:

- Target transferable skills—communication, customer service, and sales abilities carry forward over company-specifics.
- Conduct self-assessments uncovering strengths and worker personality tests guiding decisions.
- Prioritize opportunities that allow learning diverse applications from early exposure.
- Consider both immediate income needs plus long-term field prospects when selecting.
- Structure schedules balancing workload amid other commitments like academics.
- Prepare professionally—create resumes, practice interviews, learn email etiquette.
- Ask friends, parents, and teachers for company or hiring leads from networks.
- Search sites like Indeed and idealist.org for matches, then directly apply.
- Be persistent in following up on applications and tolerating some rejection.
- Accept beneficial roles seeking significance beyond just paychecks.

Before applying anywhere, do some soul-searching on your natural talents and interests too. I suggest taking free career tests, such as *YourFreeCareerTest.com* or *CareerExplorer,* that unveil your worker archetype strengths and suggest directions. Discover your power combo! Then target first jobs that align with your passions and purpose; you'll wake up already motivated.

Landing Your First Job: The Bigger Picture

I still vividly remember when my comic book and pizza cravings started dramatically outpacing the modest allowance I received in high school. By the second week of each month, I'd already blown through those funds. So, I always needed to beg my dad to spot me some cash to fund my recreational activities.

While appreciative of the lifeline, repeatedly asking my parents to bail me out took a toll on my adolescent pride and sense of financial freedom. When the neighborhood grocery store hired students, a light bulb went off—why keep relying on handouts to fund fun when I could earn my own spending money?

Landing that weekend gig proved transformative. I gained independence and no longer pleaded with my parents for small purchases. Working with older coworkers instilled a tireless work ethic, professionalism, and accountability. Handling customer complaints sharpened communication skills and empathy.

Budgeting earnings toward goals awakened my future vision—suddenly, I could work and save for grander gadgets and causes through purposeful effort.

Most importantly, earning a paycheck made me feel capable of charting my financial path forward as a young woman. That grocery store job marked a pivotal point, shaping my career and income trajectory through the power of diligent work.

CAREER VERSUS JOB

What's the difference between a career and a short-term job? While temporary jobs are mainly about earning income and trying new fields, a career aligns more closely with your long-term goals, education path, skills, and, yes, interests, too, ideally.

Some careers offer substantially more advancement growth plus higher earning potential over decades of commitment versus shorter-term jobs. Evaluate how different jobs and careers match your personal priorities, such as:

- income goals
- chances to learn new skills continually over many years
- ability to pursue work you find consistently purposeful as your interests develop
- work/life balance considerations and more

Aligning those personal priorities more tightly to a lasting career choice rather than a short-lived job is key to long-term happiness. However, this doesn't mean temporary jobs are bad. If you are acquiring new skills along the way, or if it would help boost your journey toward your goals, then don't be deterred from taking such jobs.

	Job	Career
Pay	Primarily for short-term needs	Long-term growth potential
Duration	Switches roles routinely	Sticks with industry vertical
Skills	Lacks specialization	Developed expertise over the years
Satisfaction	Just to make ends meet	Aligns with interests for Joy
Identity	Defines you by Income	Defines you by purpose
Impact	Little influence	Leadership expands reach
Evolution	Stagnates over time	Progresses into new levels

Career Questions That Need Answers

Still unsure of long-term career pursuits? Asking the right reflective questions illuminates the best-fitting paths for you. Consider the following:

- What industries seem interesting? Tech? Hospitality? Landscaping?
- Which school subjects or hobby skills come naturally that could transfer over? Math? Creative writing? Athletic abilities?
- What work environments would motivate you every day? Outdoors? Startup launches? Laboratories?
- What impact do you want your work to have? Healing people? Problem-solving? Bringing joy through entertainment?
- If all jobs suddenly paid identically, what career fields would you still gravitate toward?
- Will the career path require additional training, such as vocational certification or a 4-year college degree? This may influence decisions as well.

- Conduct informational interviews or job shadowing with contacts who are happily working in aspirational vocations, seeking their hard-won career advice. People love guiding teens!

There we have it—from the first job fit to securing career purpose, feel equipped to move toward meaningful work and get paid!

ENTREPRENEURSHIP

Teens are incredibly innovative, as demonstrated by these real-life success stories of young entrepreneurs. Consider these real-world examples of peer entrepreneurs already achieving life-changing outcomes, like six-figure incomes, before adulthood! Their stories can inspire any readers to take entrepreneurial leaps aligned with their passions.

Moziah Bridges, Mo's Bows

At age 9, Moziah ("Mo") Bridges taught himself to sew bow ties after being constantly mistaken for an adult based on his fondness for snappy suits. What began selling handmade bow ties to neighbors in his Memphis community for $15 eventually grew into a booming handcrafted menswear business grossing $200k annually by 2019—complete with licensing deals, a book release, and even White House recognition (U.S. Chamber of Commerce, n.d.)!

Alina Morse, Zollipops

When Alina confronted unhealthy eating habits exacerbating her acid reflex as a 7-year-old, her dentist father helped develop a sugar-free natural lozenge. Leveraging his industry expertise plus $7,500 in personal savings, Alina officially launched "Zollipops" from the family garage, soon striking distribution deals with massive chains like Whole Foods and 7-Eleven. Thanks to a clever teenage founder, projected sales now hover around $10 million (Sowa et al., 2019)!

STEP-BY-STEP GUIDE TO STARTING A BUSINESS

Starting a business is no easy feat. However, as you've seen, it can be done. All you need is a game plan:

1. **Identify needs and problems:** Observe trends/voids around your community tied to solutions. Maybe friends complain about limited teen event options or a lack of courier services. Perhaps parents require lawn help and professors seek research aids.
2. **Brainstorm solutions:** Next, brainstorm business offerings or products that address discovered needs, wants, and problems. For example, if your neighborhood had an overgrown lawn problem, then envision starting your mowing lawns business, or if you have a set of skills that are in demand, you could offer it and get paid in exchange.
3. **Validate Interests:** Before investing heavily, interview representatives of your target buyer groups, gauging if they would realistically become paying customers. Ask for brutally honest feedback!
4. **Draft business plans:** Outline core details like services/products offered, operations, and marketing game plans centered around validated concepts from the previous step.
5. **Fund-raise capital:** With your proof-of-concept business plans ready, you can obtain startup funding through loans, crowd-sourcing sites, or local investor events.

6. **File registration paperwork:** Formally establish your business as a legal entity with state/federal requirements like licenses, permits, and tax protocols.

And voila—your fully framed minimal viable business awaits launching! Manage challenges leaning on mentors as you build onwards and upwards.

RELEVANT BUSINESS IDEAS FOR YOU!

Unsure which concepts ultimately offer the best income upside? Consider these 20 diverse yet realistic business options customized for teen strengths:

- Freelance content writer: Blog or ghostwrite articles leveraging writing capabilities.
- Social media manager: Strategize influencer campaigns monetizing Gen Z digital instincts.
- App developer: Code basic mobile apps, solving peer problems.
- Online reseller: Buy underpriced goods locally for resale profits.
- Pet care services: Walk dogs, board animals, or train obedience.
- Lawn and yard work: Classic manual labor like mowing and raking leaves.
- Errand runner: Complete miscellaneous tasks or deliveries as a neighborhood "courier."
- Used textbook reseller: Sell gently used books to classmates.
- Online thrift store: Buy and sell pre-owned fashion.
- Voice acting gigs: Record audio content monetizing vocal talents.

- Food or craft vendor: Sell homemade goods at local events.
- Photographer/Videographer: Capture professional moments as a "media expert."
- Web designer: Build sites for local small businesses.
- Tutor: Offer classmates academic help in difficult subjects.
- Baker: Provide specialty cakes, cookies, or treats on order.
- Handyman assistant: Aid repairs and yard work assembly.
- Landscaper: Assist projects like planting gardens.
- Childcare: Babysit neighborhood kids or drive to activities.
- Party/Event helper: Offer coordinating or decorating projects.
- Mover helper: Safely assist families or older adults with lifting moves.

Many such entrepreneurial side hustles uniquely suit go-getter teen work ethics and flexibility around other obligations like schooling. Congratulations! You now know many ways to earn money while searching for or planning your dream career. Talk about turning passions into profits!

WHY TRY NEW THINGS?

Exposure to fresh activities and interests defines coming of age! Beyond just scrolling TikTok, testing unexplored experiences expands perspectives, builds character, and clarifies passions. I'm talking about everything from new sports, crafts, or summer programs to volunteering totally unfamiliar jobs. But fear of missing out (FOMO) shouldn't justify doing things recklessly either!

Career Exploration Benefits

Similar logic applies when contemplating future career fields, too. Rather than declare lifelong callings early, expose yourself to diverse professional roles by job shadowing, multi-tasking, taking internship roles, or interviewing industry veterans about their ups and downs.

Vocational sampling simply builds more well-rounded judgment through examining environments first-hand beyond idealized perceptions from afar. Interning at your lawyer dad's downtown firm may provide baller status, rubbing elbows with elite execs over catered lunch meetings.

Getting hands dirty builds crucial self-awareness, which helps clarify conditions and optimize your fulfillment, growth areas, and workplace culture fit. Ultimately, testing career scope variety before making life-altering college major investments can help sustain motivation for the long work decades ahead, drawing strength from wisdom, rather than hype.

WRITING A RESUME TO LAND YOUR FIRST JOB

A resume is a formal document summarizing one's professional qualifications and experiences for prospective employers. Crafting an impactful resume is critical when seeking that crucial first job.

The importance of a resume stems from it often being the first impression a job applicant makes. Well-presented resumes showcase skills, achievements, and competencies in a compelling overview.

This allows employers to assess if a candidate potentially fits their needs quickly. Additionally, strong resumes boost one's competitiveness during the job-hunting process. They advertise capabilities beyond what is obvious from academic credentials alone. This edge is especially important for teens with minimal formal work histories.

Building a Resume

1. When creating a resume for that crucial first job, you should highlight any relevant skills or experience that will appeal to potential employers. Even if you are without a formal work history, emphasize your strengths like responsibility, teamwork, and quick learning ability.

2. List any informal jobs like babysitting, lawn mowing, or tutoring. Use dynamic verbs to underscore abilities: "Created summer curriculum educating three elementary students in math and science" or "Coordinated schedules and transportation for five families as a reliable neighborhood babysitter." Quantify any earnings or hours worked.

3. Include academic achievements, volunteer work, and extracurricular activities. For example, "Earned high honor roll 2016-2020, maintaining 4.0 GPA while competing on the varsity tennis team." Such pursuits demonstrate time management, dedication, and other valuable soft skills.

4. Highlight technical aptitudes like programming proficiencies. Consider creating an online portfolio showcasing exemplary school or personal projects.

5. For the resume format, stick to one page. Lead with a Career Objective or Summary section explicitly stating interest and suitability for intended roles. Use consistent reverse chronological order across the Experience and Education sections.

6. Beyond content, carefully polish writing and presentation. Craft clear, concise statements with no grammar, spelling,

or punctuation errors. Use consistent verb tenses, clean fonts, and ample white space for visual appeal.

This image is an example of resume showing a possible layout. Most word processors have templates for resumes you can use to get started!

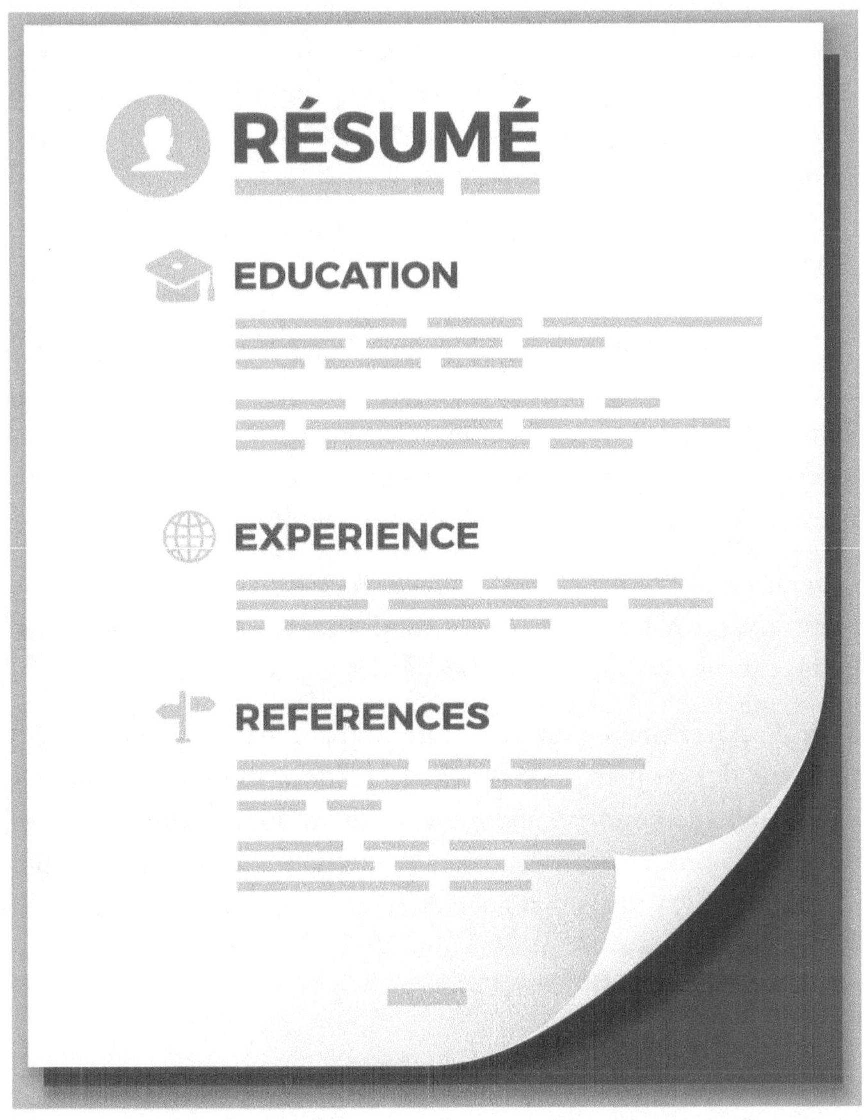

UNCLE SAM: THE GOVERNMENT WANTS YOUR MONEY

You will meet Uncle Sam soon if you earn money in the U.S. He asks every citizen to fund public projects. Roads, parks, schools, and more rely on tax dollars. If you're not in the U.S. look up the tax rules that apply to you.

We will learn who Uncle Sam taxes and why. You will understand how filing taxes works. My goal is to empower you. Taxes should not confuse you. You can master smart money moves. We will learn to respond when Uncle Sam asks you to pay taxes. Let's study income tax basics step-by-step!

Why Taxation Matters

You have heard about taxes, right? Taxes are mandatory fees charged by the government when money exchanges hands. Different taxes apply to income, sales, properties, and more. This lesson focuses specifically on income taxes targeting earnings. Income taxes are payments to the government each year.

Federal taxes are paid to *Washington D.C.* for the whole country. State taxes, on the other hand, fund your local state programs. Cities can also tax people and businesses located there.

Why do governments make citizens and companies pay taxes? All those tax dollars help build roads and schools, support the military protecting the country, and provide many more public services used by communities. Without tax money, societies cannot build the important systems that help citizens thrive.

How Are Income Taxes Collected?

Employers automatically deduct federal and state income taxes from periodic paychecks year-round. This gradual "payroll tax" collection allows contributing over time rather than owing lump sums during filing season.

Payroll taxes use IRS marginal tax brackets—income ranges tied to percentage rates collected. For example, 2023 income below $11,000 has a 10% rate. Above $11,000 gets taxed at the next bracket's higher rate.

Employers estimate tax deductions using those brackets. Workers control amounts via their "withholding allowance" selected when hired.

Some people over-withhold for bigger refunds later. Essentially, they overpay and then receive IRS reimbursements when filing taxes annually.

Those with multiple income sources must file annual reconciliations comparing taxes paid against final amounts owed for fair contributions toward public infrastructure.

Net taxable incomes apply to IRS marginal federal tax bracket percentages. Added state/city taxes are calculated thereafter.

Let's Try One Example:

- Suppose you make a total income of $55,000 every year; that means your Gross Income is $55,000.
- Let's explain the step-by-step process for the sample tax calculation using an income example of $55,000:
- We start with the Gross Income from their job field—this is the total pre-tax salary amount earned. In this case, $55,000.

- Next, the Standard Deduction removes the first $12,500 from Gross Income based on tax law. This establishes the Taxable Income figure of $42,500. In order words, $42,500 is the amount Uncle Sam is allowed to touch.
- This $42,500 Taxable Income is used to calculate taxes owed. The IRS determines percentages owed based on the income falling into Marginal Tax Brackets.
- For example, the first $11,000 of income reaches the 10% bracket—meaning it is taxed at 10%. So 10% of the first $9,700 equals $970 tax from that bracket.
- The next tax bracket charges 12% to an income of $44,725. Our example has $30,800 remaining income subject to this 12% rate. So 12% of the $30,800 equals $3,696 additional tax.

If we add $970 (from the first bracket) + $3,696 (from the second bracket), it gives the Total Estimated Tax of $4,666 owed on $55,000 Gross Income after accounting for deductions and marginal rates.

Here's a summary of our calculations:

- Gross income from job: $55,000
- Standard deduction: $12,500
- Taxable income: $55,000 - $12,500 = $42,500

Here, $42,500 is used to calculate the tax owed.

- Marginal tax brackets:
- 10% owed on first $9,700
- 12% owed on the next $30,800

Taxes would be:

- 10% of $9,700 = $970
- 12% of $30,800 = $3,696
- Total estimated tax = $970 + $3,696 = $4,666

So, in this example, $4,666 represents the estimated tax amount owed on $55,000 of gross salary income based on the percentages levied across the $9,700 and $30,800 incremental brackets this total earnings amount spans.

Steps for Filing Income Tax Returns

Submitting income tax returns takes a few steps:

Get Ready:

- Gather W-2s, 1099s, and other documentation stating all income paid from every source in the prior year. The W-2 is specifically for employed people and is issued by the employer by January 31 for the previous year, while the 1099s are for self-employed people, such as freelancers.

File Taxes:

- Use tax software like TurboTax Teens to enter your income information. Or have your parents help enter your earnings if you file taxes together.
- The software automatically finds tax deductions you qualify for that reduce how much tax you owe. Answer basic questions, and the software handles the math.

- Double-check that all income and personal information looks right, then click to officially e-file your completed tax forms directly to the government IRS website.

Get Your Refund or Pay:

- It takes the IRS 2-3 weeks to process returns and check if you overpaid taxes and get money back or if you need to send the final taxes owed.
- The IRS letter will say exactly how much to pay if you owe tax money. Pay that full amount by the deadline given.
- If you see you get a sweet refund, make sure your bank account is linked to the tax software so the money is directly deposited when ready. Remember to save!
- Check your bank account around 3 weeks after filing to see that refund hit! Then celebrate by treating yourself a little for doing your taxes!

Extra Tax Filing Help

Figuring out taxes seems like confusing homework! Well, don't worry—helpful tools exist to make it easier. The IRS website irs.gov offers extensive free guidance around DIY preparation through articles, videos, forms, and instructions. Think of it as a tuition-free tax class from the pros!

Additionally, user-friendly tax software applications like popular picks TurboTax or H&R Block guide filers through an automated question flow. After entering details, the app calculates everything behind the scenes and digitally sends completed documents for you. So, while paying taxes fuels public resources, the process itself has evolved conveniently thanks to tech and Uncle Sam's manuals!

Hiring Tax Accountants

The DIY tax preparation process often suits basic teen filers. But if pursuing self-employment income, managing investments/retirement accounts, or real estate, consider hiring a tax professional for help.

Certified Public Accountants (CPAs) undergo rigorous licensing, passing taxation and finance law exams. They help:

- increase deductions to minimize the amount owed
- avoid tax pitfalls causing penalties
- decipher confusing regulations
- save time over self-filing complex returns

Google to find CPAs in your state and compare consultation fees to leverage services.

A Tough Chapter Comes to A Brilliant Finish!

Whoa! I don't know about you, but my head still spins from all those fancy tax rules Uncle Sam cooked up! But we chopped it down step-by-step, so now you have this income and tax game on the lock to get your game on without the taxman hijacking your hard-won benjamins!

We broke it all down—how you can serve up mad value in exchange for that "bag," as you say—through traditional jobs or by chasing entrepreneurial side hustles as the next Zuckerberg. We balanced understanding taxes as feeding public services benefiting communities overall, not penalizing your hustle. Think of it as investing in functions supporting us all!

Make a Difference with Your Review!

Hey awesome readers! So, you're about halfway through diving into the incredible world of "Money Skills for Modern Teens" by Prosperity Books. Are you have a blast learning about money myths, budgets, and how to make those dollars stretch? Well, guess what? Your adventure doesn't stop here; it's time to share your thoughts and make a real difference!

Imagine this: there are teens out there just like you, maybe feeling a bit lost with money, unsure about making the right choices. Your mission, should you choose to accept it, is to help them out with a super quick and easy task – leave a review for "Money Skills for Modern Teens."

According to a survey, many Americans don't have a personal budget, and over 60% live paycheck to paycheck. That's tough, right? But you and I, we can change that. Your review might just help someone start a small business, support their family, or transform their life. Imagine being part of making dreams come true!

Ready for the 'feel good' moment? Simply scan the QR code below to leave your review. It takes less than 60 seconds, and you'll be making a real impact.

By helping a faceless friend, you become part of our club, the generous reviewers' club. Welcome! You'll love the smart money moves we'll be exploring in the upcoming chapters and knowing you're making a difference, one review at a time. Now, let's get back to our exciting money journey!

PS - Did you know, sharing something valuable with others makes you even more awesome? If you believe this book will help another friend, send it their way, and let the good vibes flow!

CHAPTER SEVEN

INVESTING—GROWING YOUR MONEY

Wise spending is part of wise investing. And it's never too late to start.

— RHONDA KATZ

Jenny is a 16-year-old high school student who invested small amounts from her part-time job into stocks. She focused on companies she regularly interacts with, like Starbucks and Nike. Over the past 2 years, she has earned over $1,200 in returns! Jenny's story demonstrates the power of investing early and letting your money grow.

You needn't be 18 or a business prodigy to start investing. This chapter guides wealth building so your money blossoms into more money over time, as Jenny's did. Plus, I'll teach you what investing is, how it works, and why starting early can set you up for financial success.

Let's dig into the methods and mentalities distinguishing savers from investors on the road to financial flourishing. Fasten your seat belts for a rewarding ride into the world of investing!

INVESTING: THE PORTAL TO WEALTH

Simply put, *investing means exchanging your hard-earned dollars for ownership shares in investments like companies, real estate, and so on, hoping to make a profit. Investing is usually long-term* and offers the best results in a longer time frame.

In contrast, saving money involves setting aside income you earn rather than spending it freely each paycheck. Saving is important, but money just sits in place, earning minor interest and not necessarily growing faster than inflation. However, saving does not have the same levels of risk as investing.

Investing puts your money on rocket boosters because it gets reinvested to earn increasingly higher returns. Let your money move and work around the clock for you!

Here is a comparison of investing in stocks versus saving in a bank to show the potential:

Investing	Saving
Involves risk for potential higher rewards	Secures funds with little to no risk
Puts money into assets expected to rise in value over 5+ years	Puts money into bank accounts earning small guaranteed interest
Targets 6-10% average annual returns	$500 at 3% interest per year nets $15
Rewards patience, allowing compound growth	Withdraw money anytime, though less gains
Invest in stocks, bonds, mutual funds, real estate, etc.	Save in options like savings accounts, CDs

HOW DOES INVESTING WORK?

Investing is like planting seeds of money that can grow into a lush money tree over time. Rather than spending everything you earn now on *wants,* you strategically put some funds into *invest-*

ment vehicles that you expect will increase in value down the road.

Wait... What are investment vehicles? Investment vehicles, also called assets, refer to the structure or platform used to invest money. Some common investment vehicles include:

- **Stocks:** Stocks represent fractional ownership in a publicly traded company. Stocks allow buying partial ownership in public companies like Starbucks, Nike, and Disney that teens interact with daily. Owning stocks essentially means owning tiny pieces of brands you know and admire! Other examples include Apple, Target, Tesla, and Netflix.
- **Bonds:** Bonds represent loans issued by corporations or governments that pay interest income over time. Examples include corporate bonds from companies like AT&T, Coca-Cola, or government bonds issued by the U.S. Treasury. The issuer pays back the principal amount when the bond reaches maturity (such as in 10 years).
- **Mutual Funds:** Mutual funds allow many investors to pool their money together into one big fund. The fund is managed by financial experts who use the cash to buy a mix of different stocks.
- **ETFs (Exchange Traded Funds):** ETFs are funds that bundle together many different assets, stocks, bonds, or commodities like gold. For example, one ETF may contain a mix of tech stocks while another tracks precious metals companies.
- These fund bundles aim to match the performance of entire markets and industries. So, rather than picking individual investments yourself, you let the experts create ETFs aligning with areas you want exposure to.

- **Real Estate:** Real estate refers to land, residential and commercial properties, buildings, and structures with value. Real estate is considered an asset form of investment with tangible physical worth. As an investment vehicle, real estate involves acquiring properties, like houses, with the expectation they will increase in market value over time.

Do you love treating yourself to frappes at Starbucks? You may not know it, but you could actually own part of Starbucks one day instead of just paying them all the time. Well, investing allows you to do just that! You essentially own tiny pieces of companies you interact with in exchange for the cash you provide them upfront to grow now.

Legendary investors like Warren Buffett became billionaires by pumping funds into companies and stocks they believe will prosper over the next 10-20+ years. Patience pays off big time. Turning modest savings into a fortune is possible when you automate investing.

Investment Mechanics

You will come across many terms as you explore investing. Here are key concepts explained simply:

- **Principal** means the amount of cash you choose to invest. This is your cost basis.
- **Rate of Return** or interest rate is the percentage your investment gains or loses each year. It's usually represented as a percentage, for example, 10% per annum (per year).
- **Profit** means the amount earned from investments.

- **Interest** is profit made on an investment.
- **Compounding** is earning interest on top of interest over the years through reinvestment. Returns build off themselves, resulting in big gains in the long term.
- **Portfolio** refers to a collection of assets.

Let's see this in action. Imagine Sam invests $1,000 into Deviceful Company stock—not a real company... yet!

The principal Sam invested is $1,000. In the first year, the stock increases by 20%, earning Sam a 20% rate of return. So his $1,000 is now worth $1,200, giving him a $200 profit.

In year two, Sam's new principal is $1,200 since that is now the starting amount invested. If Deviceful stock shoots up 20% again, Sam earns 20% off $1,200, which is $240.

So, while the annual return stays at 20% yearly, Sam's capital earned grows due to compounding. Over decades, billions can be made starting from modest amounts!

It's also important to note that, with every investment comes risk. Stocks, or any assets for that matter, can also lose value, causing you to lose your investment money.

Exciting news, my friend—investing is truly accessible today! While 20 years ago, you needed thousands saved to open a fancy brokerage account, now apps allow dollar-based investing to be accessible on your phone!

For example, with as little as $5, you can download the *Acorns app* and effortlessly turn spare change from everyday purchases into a stock portfolio. I'll tell you more about apps later.

Key requirements to invest generally include:

- being a legal adult over 18 years old (to invest on your own)
- income from jobs, gifts, inheritance, and so on
- taxable brokerage account at an investment firm
- risk tolerance plan and long-view time frame
- pick assets aligned with financial life goals

Investing ties directly to skills needed for financial independence. While saving money keeps you afloat daily, investing money is key to elevating your prosperity decades later as an adult. Finding the perfect balance is key!

I'll describe a starter investment in Netflix to spark your investing mindset. You likely stream shows and movies on Netflix today. But someday, you could financially benefit from their growth!

THE IMPORTANCE OF INVESTING EARLY

Patience and persistence are key in investing, making starting early so valuable. The beauty is through ongoing contributions and compound growth, smaller dollars invested can swell dramatically decades later.

Imagine investing $2,000 at age 18. With a moderate 10% average return yearly, that lump sum would compound over 40 years until retirement around age 60 would amount to over $38,000! Waiting to start investing closer to retirement requires spending way more money to catch up.

Legendary investor Warren Buffett bought his first stock at just 11 years old! He attributes much of his billion-dollar success to investing early and holding investments for exponential growth over very long time frames.

1. Learning the investor mindset during market ups and downs helps build resilience.
2. Even smaller invested sums can compound over time, multiplying into significant wealth.
3. Allocating "play money" for testing tactics before relying on earned income reduces pressure and allows for learning from outcomes.
4. Loosening emotional ties to money helps demystify investing and dispel intimidation myths.
5. Family guidance can smooth bumpy rides and mitigate impulse panic selling during bad markets.
6. Developing a habit of monitoring portfolios and paying attention to financial media is crucial.
7. Mistakes made early on in investing cost less and provide valuable lessons at lower stakes.
8. Compounding over 30-40-year careers enables future retirement security.
9. Having investment capital that is already growing supports entrepreneurial aspirations.
10. Diversifying assets provides safer options than relying solely on income.

Clearly, investing sooner quickens wealth-building advantages over delaying exposure until traditional adulthood milestones.

Investing pays off best the earlier you plant seeds. But it's never too late to start, either!

MOM, DAD—CAN SOMEONE OPEN AN ACCOUNT FOR ME?

As a minor under 18 in most countries, you cannot legally open investment accounts or enter formal contracts solo. However, assistance from parents or guardians can propel your investing ability forward!

That's where *custodial investment accounts* come in. These empower adults to make an investing account under their name "for the benefit of" a minor until they come of age. So, it functions like a *trust fund* paying out to the assigned youth later.

The custodian, your parent, retains control until the minor beneficiary, you, reaches adulthood per legal guidelines. However, the invested assets and any investment gains legally belong to the minor from day one.

So, with custodial accounts, you steer decision-making while relying on grownups to open accounts, since brokers officially need an adult signature. By picking assets together, you both learn!

Follow this step-by-step guide to open your first custodial account:

1. Discuss goals for the account with parents/guardians. Do they support helping?
2. Research brokers, more on this later, accepting custodial accounts like *Fidelity* and *Charles Schwab*.
3. To open an account, the adult will provide their account funding, Social Security Number, and Identity card while marking you as a beneficiary.
4. After careful research, select investment vehicles of your choice, such as ETFs, stocks, and mutual funds.
5. You can make recurring automatic contributions from your parent bank account or income.

6. When you turn 18+, the account assets can be transferred fully to you!

BROKER AND BROKERAGE ACCOUNT

Brokerage accounts let you conveniently buy and sell investments like stocks, bonds, and mutual funds in one place—just like supermarkets sell different foods.

Rather than directly contacting Apple or the NY Stock Exchange, you go through brokerages like *Fidelity* and *Charles Schwab*. The brokerage provides a digital "storefront" offering investments from various markets.

Brokers are middlemen facilitating trades, like supermarket employees, who manage product transactions between companies and shoppers.

While old-fashioned Wall Street stockbrokers manually matched buyers and sellers, today's brokerages use sophisticated digital apps and algorithms so you can seamlessly self-direct trades in your account.

TOP INVESTING APPS

Innovative financial apps make investing more accessible by allowing you to get started directly from your phone with small dollar amounts. This lets you potentially benefit from long-term market returns over time.

Here are 3 top-rated investing apps to easily build your first portfolio diversified across stocks and bonds.

Fidelity Youth Account

The Fidelity Youth Account offers 13-17 year olds hands-on investment and banking experience. You fully control the low-cost brokerage account to save, invest, and spend, while parents retain oversight capabilities.

Opening an account earns a $50 signup bonus through engaging with the investment app. No minimums, monthly fees, or domestic ATM charges exist.

While parents must approve transactions, you independently direct investments from approved stocks, ETFs, and Fidelity funds. However, certain higher-risk assets are restricted. Useful money management education resources help guide decisions.

Upon turning 18, accounts transition into standard Fidelity brokerages, retaining assets and history. Until then, parents can view all activities and statements, plus cancel cards. While more controlling than custodial accounts, Youth Accounts grant accountable independence.

Acorns

The Acorns app effortlessly saves and invests spare cash automatically in the stock market.

It rounds up everyday bank/card spending to the next dollar—those few extra pennies get invested. For example, spend $4.50 on V-Bucks, 50 cents added to savings. Over time, serious money stacks up in your investment portfolio across purchases.

Acorns create a personalized stock/bond fund mix based on your risk preferences. For most teens, it's mostly stocks since you have years ahead before needing the money—brands like Apple, Netflix, and so on. Over decades, added monthly cash and stock growth have led to nice profits.

The $1-5 monthly fees seem high compared to competitors. But overall, Acorns conveniently grows your money in autopilot mode. While nicer interfaces or bonus perks exist elsewhere, if round-ups make you save more, stopping money leaks now pays off big time later (Tepper, 2021)!

EarlyBird

EarlyBird offers a unique way for parents and families to invest gift money for a child's future rather than physical presents. You open a tax-advantaged custodial investment account with expertly managed portfolios aligned to their age.

After entering the child's info, select among five strategies from bond-heavy allocations preserving funds to equity ETFs pursuing higher long-term growth.

This intuitive app shows the current balance, projected future value at 18, recent contributor activity, contributions history, and video gift messages. Easily set recurring or one-off deposits.

Reasonable asset-based pricing means $1/month plus $2 processing per non-custodian transaction. The set-it-and-forget automated approach makes securing children's financial future straightforward for parents less comfortable personally managing market exposure. Even modest, consistent gifts can compound over 18+ years (Perez, 2020).

HOLD YOUR HORSES, DON'T INVEST JUST YET!

Before tapping "buy" on your friend's hot stock pick, pause and evaluate if investing currently suits you. Money trees topple when planted in poor soil, unprepared to receive them.

Alan lost $2,000 after hastily purchasing hyped-up crypto without researching. He broke a key rule—never risk unaffordable losses!

The coin was a Ponzi scheme fraud. Founders faked press and paid influencers to dupe first-time investors into the worthless crypto before disappearing with $30 million.

Alan went wrong by investing in hype alone without evaluating risks, credibility, or the product itself. He took on extreme risks beyond his tolerance and used crucial college savings. He wholly traded on speculation rather than fundamentals.

While Alan learned the hard way, his experience shows why upfront education and self-assessment are key. Evaluating risk tolerances, timelines, and goals preempts emotion-based decisions, which often end poorly. Always scrutinize sources and research options fully first.

No rewards come without risks, but rash investing without self-awareness fails. Disciplined patience compounds earnings from market fluctuations when rooted in understanding.

Strategically Growing Teen Wealth

Consistency builds wealth slowly but surely. Automatically put part of your money into savings before spending on random stuff. Pay yourself first!

Like putting $10 from every allowance check or paycheck into your investment account every month without fail. Then, leave it alone to grow. It's almost like a bill you owe to your future self.

Over many years, that invested stash can swell shockingly large even from modest regular additions. All you have to do is allow the wonder of *compound interest* to work magic! Not important to fully grasp now—just know consistency and time are key.

Some investment schemes pay you profits over a period of time; for example, stocks can pay you a special type of interest called dividends. Dividends are usually paid yearly and in proportion to the number of stocks you have. Rather than jumping to spend the returns on investment, you can reinvest. Use the profit to buy more assets automatically rather than cashing out payments.

BUT MOM, ALL MY MONEY'S IN FACEBOOK STOCK!

Do you know how eggs quickly break if packed into just one flimsy bag? Investing your money exclusively into a single company equates to an easily cracked portfolio, too!

Instead, diversify wisely by owning various investments across different industries, company sizes, and even countries—basically any categories possible.

Diversification means strategically spreading money among multiple assets rather than solely Apple or Tesla shares. Blend blue chip corporations, real estate income, commodity metals, cryptocurrencies, and so on to widen bases, stabilizing overall long-term values.

Say you start coming into some money through gifts, jobs, and so on and have accumulated your first $1,000 to invest; you could split across 4 areas:

1. Stocks
2. Real Estate
3. Bonds
4. Precious Metal Commodities

For example, you could invest:

- $400 in stocks
- $300 in Real Estate
- $200 in Bonds
- $100 in Cryptocurrency

Let's break this down:

Stocks: You invest the largest portion, $400, into companies positioned to grow, like Apple, Disney, and Starbucks. The key is to have some assurance because these companies are well-known worldwide and less likely to fail. Get the point?

Real Estate: Put $300 into a portfolio of properties like apartments, hotels, and warehouses. Real estate is a little risky but offers great promise.

Bonds: $200 goes to an "intermediate" investment-grade corporate bond fund that holds business debt and reliably pays interest owed. More safety than stocks.

Cryptocurrency: For $100, you can try something that's more risky but offers great potential. Cryptocurrency is one option, but do your research first since it's so new!

It doesn't have to be the above; your *portfolio* could spread your cash into investments vehicles differently with customization. It's all up to you! Many apps give suggestions.

Look up a few you might be interested in and list them here:

____

____

____

Even with diversity, investments may still lose money sometimes. What if the whole market drops severely, like the Great Recession? Spread-out assets sink, too. Owning too many random assets can lower returns compared to going "all in" on a rising standout winner like Netflix recently.

Summary

Congratulations on starting your investing journey! You now understand strategic wealth growth through owning business shares. Investing puts money into assets growing over time, generating wealth.

Start small and early, tapping into compound growth for decades. Use apps to simplify—turn spare change into fractions of mega brands.

Stay focused on long-term goals, not daily shifts. Strategically reinvest all earnings. With patience and grit, modest savings swell tremendously. But self-awareness prevents mistakes—know your risk tolerance and timeline. Research thoroughly, too.

Kudos for prioritizing financial literacy this early, compounding advantages for decades ahead! The next milestone is crafting an intentional personal financial plan before putting hard-earned dollars into markets.

So next, let's explore essential financial planning basics: Plot your course clearly to enable investing success! Knowing how to budget, save, and set retirement goals sets a good foundation for life's stability.

CHAPTER EIGHT

FINANCIAL PLANNING— ACHIEVING FINANCIAL INDEPENDENCE

The easiest way to manage your money is to take it one step at a time and not worry about being perfect.

— RAMIT SETHI

I babysat every weekend to buy stylish Jordans, only to ruin them in a single afternoon. Spending six paychecks on sneakers that would soon lose their value was a complete waste. I didn't realize then that smart money management requires continuous effort, not just a one-time sprint.

I only planned for immediate satisfaction from sneakers without considering long-term career growth. I could have also budgeted for music equipment to develop my producer side hustle or invested in retirement savings at the same time.

Mobilizing around multiple financial goals requires planning for short-, mid-, and long-term desires and then taking small steps to achieve complete financial success. Remember the "M" in our PRIME method?

There's no judgment on past mistakes; we've all been there! This chapter focuses on moving forward by creating personalized financial goals and step-by-step budget plans to master money for good, strategically. Who's ready to turn solid financial plans into future success? Let's start planning and taking action!

WHY WE NEED FINANCIAL GOALS

A financial goal is a specific money-related target that helps guide our decisions and directs our savings and spending. For example, I need $2,000 for college applications by December, or, I need to save $5,000 in total by 2025 for study abroad programs.

Having clear financial goals, like checkpoints on a long journey, are important because they help us:

- make mindful money decisions aligned with what matters most rather than impulse splurges.
- break down big intimidating targets, like affording college, into step-by-step mini-goals that feel achievable.
- create money action plans across different areas of life like lifestyle, relationships, health, and career.

Let's walk through an example:

Janelle, 17, is already stressed about paying her dream college tuition plus studying abroad in Spain. Rather than shutting down, she makes a multi-year financial plan for each phase from high school into college:

- The short-term goal is to save $2,500 in a year through babysitting to cover deposits by setting a start budget and saving 20% of earnings.

- For mid-range, research scholarships, and work programs to fund school abroad during Junior year applications.
- Lastly, long-term. Start small $50 monthly investments using graduation gift money, increasing once she has a campus job to compound gains over 2-3 years.

Janelle's spending now has a purpose—budgeting, disciplined saving, investing growth for future dreams across each year, starting from budgeting, to long-term stock market gains. Overwhelming costs feel achievable, breaking them into bite-sized budgeted actions today while her funds grow toward the future.

From above, you'll find themes discussed in previous chapters: Budgeting, savings, investments, and now a financial plan.

TYPES OF FINANCIAL GOALS

Financial goals generally fall into 3 buckets depending on priority timelines:

Short-Term Goals: Less than 1 year

Short-term financial goals focus on urgent needs or financial obligations already incurred. This includes building a starter emergency fund, paying off recent debts interfering with cash flow, and covering upcoming essential expenses.

Think basic safety nets first. Examples:

- saving $500 in a Secure Savings Account over 6 months
- paying off $200 owed for car repair by August
- budgeting $800 for textbook costs next semester

Mid-Range Goals: 1-5 years

Medium-term financial goals refer specifically to the time frame of 1-5 years. They fill the gap between urgent short-term needs and long-horizon dreams.

Goals set with a medium-term, or 1-5 year time frame have enough breathing room to make significant financial progress while still being achievable relatively soon.

Examples:

- gaining a social media marketing certificate by 2025 to increase salary.
- maintaining credit card payments on time over 3 years to achieve credit for a future dream apartment
- transitioning side hustle blog into profitable personal finance site

Long-Term Goals: Over 5 years

Long-term financial goals fund the big bucket list of dreams that require an extended savings time frame of 5+ years. We're talking home ownership, expanding that dream career path, taking luxury vacations, and achieving financial independence to retire early.

Examples:

- saving $80k total toward $100k down payment on first home by 2030
- building a $500k investment portfolio by 2045 for early retirement adventures
- backpacking through Europe for a one-year sabbatical in 2038

With some brainstorming on short, medium, and long aims meaningful for you, how can financial goals guide your money decisions toward exciting milestones ahead?

CREATING YOUR MONEY VISION BOARD

What does financial success look like to you—rich and fancy, travel-filled adventure, a stable future home base? However you picture your money dreams, I'm here to make those visions a reality!

Let your imagination run wild for a second. If money limitations didn't hold you back, what goals and treats would spark that joy for you now and years from now? Really sit with it and get curious about what you want.

What if I told you the power to make those monetary dreams real is already within you?

I'm not talking about magic genies here. This is about finally taking control of your money story—through smart goal-setting and commitment.

I want you to stop dreaming about financial freedom and start actively creating it—your vision and rules.

We'll make it happen through an activity I call the Money Vision Board. Using magazines, markers, goals, and dreams—you will build a personalized vision board that maps your financial targets out creatively. This thing will fire you up every single time you see it.

Then, over time, you'll watch those dreams go from paper to reality by revisiting this board and setting clear money action plans. I'll walk you through making this vision board pop and share tips to actualize it.

Instructions:

1. Cut out inspiring images, words, and quotes from magazines and newspapers that capture your financial goals and dreams— both short and long-term. Get creative!

2. On a poster board or blank canvas, neatly arrange and glue these visual elements however you wish to design your own money vision board.

3. Now, using sticky notes or writing directly on the board, map your ideas and targets to these visual elements by answering the following:

- What does this goal mean to you, and why does it matter?
- How much money do you need for this and by what date?
- What first step can you take toward this in the next week?
- What obstacles may arise, and how will you push through?
- Who can support you in staying motivated?
- How will achieving this make you feel? Visualize already having reached it.

4. Proudly display your Money Vision Board somewhere you'll see it daily for inspiration and accountability. Revisit it often to refresh your financial targets and timelines as life changes. Update the targets and add new motivational images or quotes as needed.

Image used with permission from Darmoroz at iStock.

Awesome job creating your Money Vision Board! Now, it's time to make those dreams come true. Of course your example will include more detailed money information than the image above!

I will walk you through mapping action plans to turn each vision board item into reality. We'll capture the small steps that will compound over time into big success if you stick with it.

Here's how to create your strategic money road map:

For each goal visual on your board:

1. **Name It:** Give this specific dream a title. Write it at the top of a notebook page—something like "Trip to Japan" or "Professional Camera Gear."

2. **Timeline:** Decide on your target savings amount and date. Even if it's 10 years away, note it—this gives your brain a destination to work toward.
3. **Break It down:** Brainstorm smaller milestone sub-goals that build monthly and year to year, helping you hit that ultimate target. Consider saving $100 monthly for a trip or selling used items to fund gear.
4. **Crunch Numbers:** Use a compound interest calculator to estimate what consistent monthly saving could yield years later—and experiment with accelerating sub-goal amounts over time as income rises.
5. **Name Obstacles:** Job changes, recessions, unexpected bills —note external events that may knock you off course. Then, problem-solve backup plans to adapt.
6. **Seek Supporters:** List any friends, mentors, or sites that can keep you motivated, troubleshoot obstacles, and so on. Reach out and activate your team.
7. **Reminders:** Add calendar alerts for bi-yearly check-ins. Update target amounts and timelines as life shifts. Consistency is key!

Do this detailed plan for each vision board item. By naming the micro and macro goalposts, your brain can structure efficient money action plans customized to your dreams.

JADA SETS HER GOALS

Meet Jada, 16. Inspired after creating her Money Vision Board displaying dreams of seeing a concert in NYC, buying a used car, and retiring early to a lake house, she's ready to make plans.

Jada starts by detailing 3 goals across time frames:

Short-Term Goal (1-2 years)

Name: Springsteen VIP Concert and NYC Trip.

Details: Experience a premium Springsteen concert with backstage access in New York City in the summer of 2025.

Total Cost: $5,000 for tickets, travel, hotels.

Target Date: August 2025.

Action Plan: Monthly Savings Required: $208 ($2,500/yr over 2 years).

Date	Milestone Goal	$ Amount	Total Saved
March 2024	Birthday money from gifts	$500	$500
June 2024	Babysitting 2x/week	+$100/month ($1,200/yr)	$1,700
January 2025	Ask for concert tickets as only bday gift	$1,000 value	$2,700
April 2025	Sell collectibles on eBay	$500	$3,200
June 2025	Part-time summer job	$1,800	$5,000

Don't get anywhere near $500 for a birthday gift? That's ok, you can make goals on any budget, may take time and creativity to achieve them. They key is having the money smarts you are learning now!

Medium-Term Goal (3-5 years)

Name: Used Hybrid Car Purchase.

Details: Buy a used, reliable hybrid sedan for college to reduce gas costs.

Total Cost: $15,000.

Completion Date: June 2027.

Date	Milestone Goal	$ Amount	Total Saved
January 2024	Birthday gifts	$500	$500
Monthly	Part-time job	$150/month x 36 months	$5,400
June 2025	Cash graduation gifts	$2,000	$7,400
December 2025	Sell stock inherited from an aunt	$5,000	$12,400
Summer Months	Seasonal resort job	$2,600	$15,000

Long Term Goal (10+ years)

Name: Lakefront Cabin Retirement.

Details: Purchase lakefront cabin to retire early in—paid in cash.

Total Cost: $750,000.

Target Date: 60th birthday (2070)—44 years from now!

Monthly Investing Required: $156.25 monthly, increasing 5% per year.

Start Year	Monthly Investment	Annual Contribution	Total Saved (with 12% Return)
2024	$156.25	$1,875	$1,875
2025	$164	$1,968	$3,995
2026	$172	$2,061	$7,433
2027	$181	$2,166	$11,288
...	...	...	...
2070	$5,097	$61,164	$1,350,000

Jada reviews her detailed action plans, breaking each goal into manageable money milestones over time. She gets excited seeing all the steps to turn her dreams into reality—whether small, consistent savings, gifts, jobs, or asset sales. By naming targets for her future self, Jada builds money momentum!

10 GOALS SETTING HACKS

Here are 15 tips for you to keep in mind when setting and working toward your financial goals:

1. Automate deposits into a dedicated savings account directly from each paycheck.
2. Set realistic deadlines for incremental milestone steps toward your final savings goal.
3. Clearly define the precise target savings amount and what expenses it will be used for.
4. Share your savings goal with friends to recruit motivational allies.
5. Explore negotiating a raise, adding shifts, or side hustles to actively boost income.
6. Anticipate obstacles that may derail savings efforts and draft contingency plans to adapt.

7. Acknowledge and celebrate achieving smaller milestones that indicate progress.
8. Have an impulse savings plan to leverage unexpected windfalls like bonuses.
9. Use visual trackers to watch savings grow tangible over time.
10. Prioritize "paying yourself first" savings from each paycheck before other costs.

A FINANCIAL PLAN: THE GRAND DREAM

A financial plan is a comprehensive long-term strategy for managing your financial life across all money matters. It involves your plans for:

- earning money.
- managing your expenses.
- saving.
- investing.
- paying insurance.
- filing taxes.
- retirement.

It projects your financial future across decades and guides both big-picture and detailed money decisions.

Components of a Financial Plan

- **Income streams:** Document all current and expected future sources of income from jobs, gifts, allowances, side hustles, investment returns, and so on, and anticipate timeline changes.
- **Expense budgeting:** Track spending today across categories like food, entertainment, transportation, housing, utilities, clothing, and so on. Project future costs in retirement or if major life changes occur.
- **Emergency and regular savings:** Calculate ideal savings target amounts both for unexpected costs short-term and expected future purchases like vehicles, homes, and long-term vacations.
- **Banking and debt management:** Select banking and loan products optimal for your cash flows and interest costs, integrating mortgages, credit cards, and student loan repayments.
- **Investing strategies:** Research different investment vehicles and develop an automated strategy balancing risk tolerance, timelines, and compounding returns.

- **Insurance planning:** Determine ideal coverage types and amounts across auto, health, life, home, disability, and so on, based on assets and lifestyle risks.
- **Retirement planning:** Define your desired retirement age and lifestyle costs, then calculate the savings and investing contributions required to fund decades of not working.
- **Estate planning:** Even before retirement, outline your beneficiary selection, wills, trusts, and so on to transfer assets to heirs smoothly.

Why Financial Plans Matter for Teens

Having a clear money map early on helps you:

- establish healthy financial habits around saving and budgeting.
- strategically direct funds toward your most important short and long-term goals.
- weather unexpected expenses or income changes without spiraling into debt.
- achieve major future milestones like college, vehicle purchases, and home down payments on ideal timelines.
- maximize lifetime wealth-building potential.

The sooner you start proactively planning your finances, the more reward you reap later from the power of compounding growth in your investment and net worth.

Financial Plan vs. Financial Goals

Up until now, you've been reading about goals... goals... goals! At first, they sound similar—just some boring grown-up stuff, right? Well, listen up because knowing the difference between these two terms makes achieving your money dreams way less confusing!

Think of financial goals as mini checkpoint targets along the road toward your ultimate destination. For example, saving up to buy the latest gaming console or a car is a financial goal.

A financial plan zooms out to map your entire financial journey from start to finish, keeping those key goals on track. It combines everything—income, budget, savings, and investment accounts—into one money road map custom-designed just for you!

So, goals are bite-sized baby steps that support the bigger-picture financial plan. My job is to get you laser-focused and pumped up about each milestone while ensuring your total quest stays on track too.

Here's a summary of their key differences:

Criteria	Financial plan	Financial goals
Timeline	Life-long	Short, medium, and long term
Scope	Your whole money world	Specific targets
Includes	Jobs, spending, saving, investing, taxes... everything!	That new laptop, Europe trip fund, college pot
Purpose	Maps out overall money strategy	Lays out amounts and deadlines
Benefits	Make smart long-term choices to build wealth	Make incremental progress to key moments

ALEX'S FINANCIAL PLAN VISION BOARD

Alex knew she wanted to study marine biology one day, so she started plotting out a financial road map to get there. First, she wrote "VET SCHOOL OR BUST!" in huge bubble letters at the top —her massive money mountaintop goal.

Then, she mapped smaller milestones to make that distant dream more reachable:

- Summer job at aquarium = income stream #1 (*Draws an aquarium doodle with coins spouting out*).
- Save from every paycheck for college (*Draws a piggy bank filling up with coins*).
- Take challenging courses to earn scholarships (*Draws graduation cap and diploma*).

She's starting to see how each smaller plan supports the next. When you string enough of those mini-missions together, suddenly, you're shaking the Dean's hand and graduating debt-free!

After her initial vision board brain dump, Alex created a categorized budget to track her marine biology dreams into monthly action. She set up a spreadsheet with columns for:

Income

- Aquarium guide salary: $480/month
- Dog walking earnings: ~$100
- Birthday money gifts: $150 avg

She totaled about $730 monthly, which she could devote just to college savings! Not bad coin for a 16-year-old.

Expenses

- Gas for car: $80
- Extracurriculars: $25
- Clothes: $20

- 10% fun money: $70

Alex was honest with herself about non-negotiable real-world teenager costs. Being realistic avoids budget burnout!

Savings

- Veterinary school fund: $535/month target

Nearly 75% of earnings went straight to her future college tuition fund. Talk about dedication! But Alex visualized walking across that graduation stage, so she remained laser-focused.

Debt

No student loans for Alex! She researched scholarships early so the debt wouldn't derail her vet school plans. I showed her sites like FastWeb that match applicants with grants and financial aid opportunities. Getting free cash to fund her future—now that's a smart money saving! Don't be afraid to ask local businesses if they offer scholarships.

SIDE HUSTLES

To keep her marine biology dreams swimming, Alex got creative with seasonal side jobs that fit her interests:

Summer

- lifeguarding at the pool
- running a kids' swim camp
- doggy daycare assistant

In warm months, Alex capitalized on pet care and water fun gigs! The camp she led brought in over $1,000 just in summers.

School Year

- peer tutor in biology and math
- caring for neighbors' exotic pets when traveling
- medical scribing internship weekends

During class time, Alex offered her advanced skills up for hire! She charged $20/hour helping other students grasp tricky concepts. Cha-ching for her college fund!

Scholarship Smarts

Alex creates a master spreadsheet to track college scholarship applications—due dates, requirements, and amounts. With so many options, organization was key! Thanks to her focused efforts, she scored 2 full-ride academic scholarships—that's free tuition, folks!

When her spreadsheet flowed red into the negative or life threw surprise expenses her way, she reworked the numbers, often with her parents. Her parents helped Alex identify seasonal side hustles to amp up income, like tutoring around exams or pet holiday photoshoots to bridge short-term money gaps.

The key for her was balancing realistic everyday teen spending while maximizing college cash flow. Having her eyes on the prize kept her monthly money motivation high, even through sacrifices!

You Can Do It, Too!

Where do you want your financial path to lead years from now? Targeted goal-setting and planning turn lofty monetary dreams into reality.

First, differentiate short-term impulse buys from mid-range milestones and lifelong aims like college or early retirement. Breaking bigger goals into doable mini-targets makes them feel achievable.

Next, create an inspirational "Money Vision Board" collage with images, quotes, drawings of future milestones, and account screenshots to bring financial dreams alive. Use sticky notes to detail the precise savings, dates, and steps to achieve each item.

Armed with visible finish lines across time frames, build road maps to get there. Name obstacles and supporters, calendar deadlines, and celebrate sub-goals reached. These practical steps, done consistently, bridge present days to future achievement.

The PRIME method's "Mobilize" stage maps strategic financial plans, turning ambitious monetary visions into profitable reality through consistent short-term actions. Time to put your future money where your mouth is!

CHAPTER NINE

BUILDING CREDIT, MINIMIZING DEBT

What can be added to the happiness of a man who is in health, out of debt, and has a clear conscience?

— ADAM SMITH

Did you know some college students and grads struggle to have money to spend money on other essential things? That's because these individuals still hold student loans. Today's teens are taking on record levels of debt—mainly from student loans, credit cards, and personal loans.

Understandably, today's teenagers feel significant pressure to take on student debt and utilize loans or credit cards without fully grasping the long-term implications. However, while an emergency line of credit can prove helpful, it comes with a cost—You have to pay back the loans and deal with interest rates.

But have no fear! While the student debt situation may look dire, this chapter will equip you to minimize and avoid debts. We'll walk through proven strategies to build your credit, dodge debt traps, and set yourself up for financial freedom.

Rather than follow past generations struggling under cycles of debt, you can master key credit concepts early. This knowledge, combined with fiscal discipline, empowers you to leverage financial tools on your way to adulthood.

WHAT IS CREDIT?

You probably hear the word "credit" tossed around a lot, but what does it actually mean, and why should you care? Here's the 101...

In simple terms, credit refers to your track record of borrowing money and repaying loans on time. Lenders report this history to credit bureaus, distilling the data into your three-digit credit score.

What's the big deal about this little number? Think of your credit score as a financial report card launching you forward or holding you back. A high grade unlocks rewards like loan approvals using other people's money!

But mess up payments or overspend, and your grade tanks, creating obstacles to financing significant purchases later—yikes! Suddenly, building responsible credit habits early becomes important to understand.

Lucky for you, establishing positive credit is straightforward when you know the secrets. Follow along as we break down key ideas and terms to set you up for current and future money wins with some tips and tricks!

MORE ON CREDIT AND CREDIT REPORT

If your financial life were a book, your credit score would be the Cliffs Notes summary used to assess creditworthiness. This three-digit number, ranging from *300 to 850,* gives lenders an at-a-glance snapshot of how reliably you are expected to pay back borrowed money based on your history. Think of them like your school grades.

But how do the credit bureaus crunch reams of transaction data into one number? And what exactly makes it go up and down? At a basic level, these 5 core aspects affect your credit score:

1. **Payment history:** Have you repaid loans and bills on time previously? Patterns over months and years are revealing.
2. **Total debt load:** How much do you owe across all accounts compared to your total borrowing limit? Risk rises as balances approach maximums.
3. **Credit history length:** How long have you shown the ability to manage different credit accounts responsibly? Generally, more years/decades are favorable.
4. **Recent credit applications:** An overload of new accounts in a short period can indicate financial over-extension even if repaid promptly. Moderation brings stability.
5. **A mix of credit types:** Experience handling loans, mortgages, credit cards, and so on demonstrates proficiency across financial products over time. Variety signals flexibility.

Based on performance across these areas, the resulting score predicts your risk of defaulting on new credit. Just like a test score, higher indicates lower perceived risk, while lower means additional financial education could be beneficial to unlock better rates.

Monitoring your reports for accuracy and maintaining helpful money management behaviors provides the study tools to ace this assessment!

The key is realizing your score dynamically reflects how reliably lenders think you can handle growing credit.

WHERE DO SCORES COME FROM?

Credit scores originate from 3 major credit bureaus: Equifax, Experian, and TransUnion. These influential companies access our long history of managing bills, loans, and debts—tracking individual financial behaviors over decades.

Then, the secretive part: They feed this payment data into complex algorithms and formulas, analyzing patterns and crunching numbers to produce our credit scores. So, while it feels random, teams of data scientists actually carefully develop the calculations.

The good news? Scores don't arise arbitrarily to torment us! Understanding the inputs—our money management histories— gives us power. We can tweak financial behaviors purposely to aim higher. While computations stay mysterious, taking charge of ourselves makes success possible. Every small money move matters when building financial freedom!

CHECKING YOUR CREDIT REPORTS

You can get free copies of your credit reports every year at annual-creditreport.com. These reports show everything that goes into calculating your scores: loan payments, credit cards, and bills over the years.

So, review the reports closely! Make sure nothing wrong or unfair is dragging your score down. Fix mistakes. Say an old bill your roommate left unpaid is still listed—not good! Send a dispute form to get errors removed fast. This doesn't have to be difficult; I'll mention some great apps that can help you manage your credit in a later section.

INTERPRETING SCORE RANGES

Ah, the ever-important score ranges: I remember feeling so lost trying to make sense of them as a teen! Let your friendly credit mentor break it down in simple terms:

800+ = Excellent

If you score above 800, go ahead and do a happy dance! That's like acing a big test with extra credit. You'll get the best deals on loans, credit cards, and apartments. Banks see little risk in lending to you, so they offer you their lowest interest rates. Party time!

700-749 = Good

Crossing that 700 threshold means you're doing great managing bills and debts overall. Lenders still view lending to you positively. You'll qualify for solid loan rates, new cards with nice perks, and reasonably priced leases. My first studio apartment acceptance letter came right after hitting 725—what a moment!

650-699 = Fair

Don't fret about being in the OK zone, friends. You might just be starting out building your credit history or overcoming past money struggles. The good news is that patiently boosting scores is very doable! For now, focus on paying bills on time every month. Watch offers roll in as you inch higher.

<650 = Poor

Scores below 650 feel frustrating, I know. Late payments sink us fast. My mom lost her job when I was young, and our scores tanked. But here's the key—don't give up! Lean on mentors, setting you up for success. Prioritize bills protecting essential needs first. Then, rebuild card-by-card. Celebrate small wins. You've so got this!

Activity: Use an app listed below to find out what your score is and put it here ___________.

WHAT IMPACTS YOUR CREDIT SCORE?

Do you know how in games, you start with a certain amount of coins? It's the same with Credit score. Everyone starts with an average score and gradually reaches for the top. One mistake, and you're going down. With poor credit, getting loans becomes difficult. That's why it's important you put your credit score in order.

Get ready for the inside scoop on what truly moves the score needle! Here are the top 3 factors:

Payment History: Bills Paid On Time?

Drumroll... this one accounts for a whopping 35%! It sounds boring, but paying all bills by the due date every month is crazy powerful. When I moved out, I taped reminders everywhere until paying on time became a habit. And you can't beat auto-pay set for bills, my friends. My score recently hit 790 thanks to years of auto-piloting payments.

Credit Usage: High Balances Hurt!

So, this part tripped me up for a bit. I figured using credit cards frequently was good since I paid them back on time. Wrong! Letting balances get too high for too long drags scores down, even if eventually settled. Now, I pay in full each month. Fun fact: My prom cocktail dress came from rewards points from a card I keep under 30% usage. Happy memories!

Credit History/Age: Longer Is Better

Finally, the longer your history looks responsible with credit, the better. They want to see consistent good money habits over time, not just a few months. I admit I missed payments here and there as a young teen. But about 10 years later, that old, messy history mattered much less than the years of intelligent credit moves. Time really helps! So start now!

CREDIT APPS WORTH CHECKING OUT

Who has time to constantly check credit scores with everything else going on? I get it. But critical apps now put that power right in our pockets!

I've identified the top 3 must-download credit helpers to fit anyone's situation. Just a few taps unlock tips like previewing score impacts of money moves before acting.

#1. Credit Karma

This free app is necessary for tracking scores and reports from Equifax and TransUnion whenever you want. What I love most is that they don't just show your score—the interface is visual, breaking down exactly what credit factors are helping or hurting you. As you can see, late payments drag you down 3%. Empowering!

#2. Experian

Experian lets you connect accounts like Netflix to boost your credit mix, which can lift scores. And I dig how they send timely payment reminders and updates when new accounts open in your name. Staying on top of credit feels way easier. They even offer a basic free version!

#3. CreditWise

Honestly, the gaming vibe of CreditWise makes monitoring kind of fun! You earn badges for reaching score milestones month-to-month. And the app can simulate how future moves could change your score, like paying off student loans or opening new credit. It is super helpful to see the impact ahead of time!

So there you have it—my top app picks for savvy credit users on the go. May we all cheer each other on securing brighter financial futures! Which one catches your eye?

Based on the factors affecting your score, list 2-4 ideas in the space below about what you can start doing today to improve your score:

____

____

____

____

DEBT: A FINANCE MAZE

Debt means you are *borrowing money to* purchase *something now that you otherwise could not fully afford.* You then owe repayment of that money to whoever lent it to you over an agreed period into the future—whether that be a credit card company, bank, or Uncle Sam himself when it comes to student loans!

Not All Debts Are Equal

Before you tune out at just the word "debt," let me emphasize that not all types should scare you off automatically!

Certain debts are secured by precious assets, meaning those items get tied to the loan. If you fail to repay as initially promised, the lender can legally seize your property to make up for your defaults. Still with me?

For example—shiny cars in driveways, big suburban homes, even that pallet of designer skinny jeans financed for your e-commerce shop inventory... they likely came from secured auto loans, home mortgages, and small business lines of credit with the items themselves collateralizing the borrowed amounts.

Meanwhile, unsecured debts have no specific property or assets attached—just legal obligations created entirely by signatures swearing to repay. So, while missing unsecured debt payments like credit card bills or medical expenses won't lead repossession truck drivers to show up at your front door... financial consequences still loom without pledged assets held hostage per se.

COMMON CONSUMER DEBT TYPES

Expanding on those foundations, adults' most common debts typically fall into either revolving unsecured loans or installment-secured borrowing.

Revolving debt: These optional debts can be endlessly reused up to an approved limit, and then paid down in flexible amounts and timing. It's why we lovingly call credit cards revolving doors of spending temptation! But when managed wisely, reward points also keep flowing in kind. You have got to stay balanced.

Installment loans: Debts like home mortgages, student loans, and car financing allow set amounts to be borrowed upfront, structuring required payments over multi-year periods until the balance gets eliminated. If you miss too many fixed monthly installments, though, either the collector comes calling, or assets may change hands!

Beyond the main categories of revolving (flexible balances and payments like credit cards) and installment (structured payment loans like mortgages) debts, several specific debt varieties weigh on consumers. Let's review them:

- **Credit card debt:** Money borrowed from card companies to purchase goods/services with a promise to repay by the due date. Interest and fees add up quickly if monthly balances are not paid in full.
- **Mortgage debt:** Long-term loans finance real estate purchases like houses or condos. Buyers gain ownership over time, making monthly installment payments.
- **Student loan debt:** Money borrowed to pay for higher education expenses with structured payments for years after graduation. Interest accrues during and after school.

- **Auto loan debt:** Financing allows car ownership immediately while incrementally making payments over months/years to pay it off and fully own the vehicle.
- **Small business debt:** Launching a business requires upfront money—there's no way around that funding need. But before going into any financing, be informed on exactly what a business loan will require in monthly payments and other responsibilities. Making entrepreneurial dreams a reality takes more than just a signature committing you to debt obligations. It's essential to have a thoughtful business and repayment plan in place first.
- **Medical debt:** Getting hurt or sick throws anyone's budget off badly. However, many options exist for managing costs, like payment plans or assistance programs. Talk to providers so medical needs don't turn into money knots. Help is out there!

Good Debt vs. Bad Debt

Let me tell you the story of my mentee Neha, who recently graduated. While she took out $30,000 in federal student loans to earn her degree and pursue a fulfilling career, she also racked up $5,000 on credit cards, treating friends to regular weekend shopping and partying.

Given her entry salary and existing commitment, which debt builds Neha's financial foundation versus merely funding fleeting fun now, causing payment pain later?

Bingo—strategic student loans fuel brighter lifetime income potential as *"good debt."* Meanwhile, unnecessary card balances wasted on temporary pleasures without lasting value are classified as *"bad debt."*

Good debt means borrowing money that ultimately invests in acquiring assets likely gaining value or boosting your overall income over time—like education, real estate, and starting businesses.

Bad debt *funds instant gratification purchases without financial value* or ensures payment headaches later—lavish vacations, delivered meals, and Instagram-worthy clothes bought on money you don't have yet. It's fun when swiping cards but not so much when minimum payments come due!

Why Avoid Bad Debt?

Bad debt earns its nasty reputation because of compounding interest, paying interest on interest, causing balances to balloon over time, and stealing freedom to save money for other goals. And with no added assets or increased income for all those hefty interest payments, bad debt creates relentless stress!

What Makes Good Debt So "Good"?

Borrowing money doesn't have to trap you in vicious financial cycles without end. The benefits far outweigh temporary payment burdens by strategically assuming good debt, boosting your net worth, or unlocking higher earning power like Neha's useful university studies.

Mortgages showcase how borrowing strategically with good debt can work to your benefit. Financing a home instead of paying the full price in cash gives you the advantage of property appreciation over time.

As the home's value rises beyond just your principal payments, that extra equity pads your overall investment. Letting increasing housing prices offset some of the mortgage debt over decades transforms borrowing into a leverage tool that builds wealth.

What Debt Does to You

We must acknowledge that, left unchecked, any debts snowballing out of control thanks to high interest eventually take a toll. Bombarded by collectors, succumbing further to ballooning balances, and perpetually putting payments ahead of living life with any financial freedom, is certainly no way to thrive!

Psychological and emotional health inevitably suffers. Relationships are strained. Savings are entirely deprived to invest toward dreams or even emergency needs. The reckless debt cycle certainly gives nothing back long-term compared to strategic good debt boosting your stability.

Seek out mentors if needed, get savvy on interest calculations, and find your future freedom by first understanding debt. We'll get through any challenges together, one step at a time!

DEBT AND YOUR CREDIT SCORE

Let's reevaluate those critical three digits—your credit score—representing years of debt management behaviors. Messing up payments and letting debts overwhelm finances tanks scores faster than my wannabe TikTok dances fail to go viral.

And bad credit doesn't just randomly happen with irresponsible adulthood. It directly restricts opportunities—from qualifying for apartments and car loans to accessing the best phone plans or travel rewards cards. In other words, bad credit limits your chances to move and grow money. And money momentum fuels nearly every dream these days!

Remember the PRIME method for financial literacy, including budgeting, saving, investing in yourself, planning, and adapting? The "M" stands for "Money," and responsible debt and credit play into that.

So be vigilant in giving lenders their dollars on time. Think twice before swiping cards for short-term escapes over long-term goals. And speak up for mentorship when challenges hit, and scores slip. We'll turn credit woes around together and get you primed for the life you deserve.

7 HOT TIPS FOR GETTING OUT OF AND AVOIDING DEBT

If you feel weighed down by the heavy weight of debt, here are some great tips that even professionals follow to clear their debts:

1. **Pause all cards:** Freeze spending on credit cards immediately by cutting them up and buying essentials with cash only.
2. **List debts from smallest to largest:** Write out all debts regardless of interest rate from the smallest balance owed to the largest.
3. **Pay minimums on all debts:** Continue paying minimum amounts due on all debts to avoid late fees and credit damage.
4. **Funnel extra money to smallest debt:** Throw any spare cash at the smallest debt on your list to wipe it out quickly.
5. **Repeat as debts get paid off:** As you eliminate each small debt, roll that minimum payment toward attacking the next most significant debt.
6. **Use the small debts first:** Making the smallest debts disappear first clears room to funnel those minimum payments toward the next most significant balance when

freed up. This debt payment strategy is called the snowball effect.

7. **Increase income where possible:** Pick up side gigs like dog walking, tutoring, or selling online to speed up the debt snowball effect.

The key is focusing on wiping out debts before spending on other goals. Once your balance avalanche lands you debt-free, it's time to breathe easier and never look back!

Level Up Your Credit Game!

This chapter covers essential debt, credit, and financial impact concepts. We discussed how contemporary students take on alarming debt without fully grasping future consequences. While some emergency credit helps, interest compounds rapidly, and debt must eventually be repaid.

We explored the differences between bad debt funding impulses versus good debt fueling investments like education. Managing credit and debt wisely early on sets positive lifetime patterns.

Additionally, credit scores represent risk levels to lenders based on repayment history, qualifying or disqualifying financial opportunities shaping lifestyle and mobility. Staying informed on score factors while building good money management habits empowers students to take control of their futures.

Now equipped with strategic debt and credit fundamentals, you have the power to shape a bright path forward. Join me next as we map out significant purchases confronting young adults and explore wise long-term savings and planning.

CHAPTER TEN

CREATING YOUR FUTURE— UNDERSTANDING BIG EXPENSES

Rebecca could hardly contain her excitement after four long years of high school and college applications. When she got that thin envelope from the Pennsylvania College of Art and Design, she almost exploded—she was going to design school! Her parents worried about the cost of taking loans, but she reassured them her graphic design skills would land her a good job after graduation.

Fast forward past orientation, dorm shopping, and tearful good-byes. Rebecca just finished her final first-year classes and is starting an internship at an excellent letterpress studio in the city. Her new graphic designer friends rave about the hip neighborhoods and apartments within walking distance of downtown. Eager for independence, Rebecca checks out some listings only to find even run-down one-bedroom apartments going for $2,000 per month!

That's way beyond the tiny stipend from her print-making apprenticeship. But she doesn't want another cramped dorm year or continue bumming rides home off-campus. Her dream apartment seems impossibly far out of reach on an entry-level budget after growing up comfortably middle class.

How can Rebecca balance her goals of launching an artistic career in the city she loves while making intelligent money decisions? What financial knowledge should she arm herself with before signing any lease?

THE BIG CHOICES

Now that you're crossing the threshold into adulthood's door, let me be the first to congratulate but also prepare you. I distinctly remember standing where you are now, dizzy with new freedom but facing down choices that felt way too big and real.

Choosing a college, buying my first clunker car, and signing a shoebox apartment lease impacted everything that came after! They changed the course of my financial life, for better and worse. So, I want you to really weigh the options and impacts before diving in based on impulse, emotion, or what your friends are doing.

Take it from me: these choices around school, vehicles, housing, and more carry huge price tags that will be on your shoulders for years. The loans and interest rack up faster than you realize. Going blind without understanding the expenses changed my entire financial path. I don't want the same for you!

That's why, in this chapter, I'll walk you through assessing your unique situation, tallying the actual costs, and exploring clever alternatives before cementing pivotal life choices. My goal is not to limit your dreams, but rather equip you to achieve them without derailing your future. The correct information now empowers you, not overwhelms you!

So, let's dig into those intimidating price tags and break down the trade-offs together, choice by choice.

The College Chase

Think back to the last YouTube review binge before purchase—you likely compared every stat! Bring that savvy energy to pick your future alma mater since it might be your first six-figure investment!

Say your school dream is a private prestigious university at $70k yearly. An excellent public college alternative might run you $30k per year. And community college is just $5k annually before transferring. These tuition figures seem straightforward enough to compare, but wait...

Don't forget room and board can bump up costs significantly. When calculating and comparing college options, you need the total price estimate.

Let's dig deeper by breaking down potential 4-year costs side-by-side for a couple of schools—from tuition, housing, and food to books, fees, and extras. Comparing total price tags better informs decision-making.

See the table template below for evaluating options. You can use this to compare the true costs of your potential colleges. An informed choice weighs your goals against numbers—saving money and time.

School Name	Private Prestige University	Solid State University	Local Community College
Tuition	$70,000 x 4 years = $280,000	$15,000 x 4 years = $60,000	$5,000 x 2 years = $10,000
Room & Board	$12,000 x 4 years = $48,000	$9,000 x 4 years = $36,000	$0
Textbooks	$1,500 x 4 years = $6,000	$800 x 4 years = $3,200	$500 x 2 years = $1,000
Fees	$2,000 x 4 years = $8,000	$500 x 4 years = $2,000	$250 x 2 years = $500
Misc. Expenses	$3,500 x 4 years = $14,000	$2,000 x 4 years = $8,000	$1,000 x 2 years = $2,000
Total Cost	**$356,000**	**$109,200**	**$13,500**

Keys:

- 4 years: The four-year study duration.
- 2 years: The two-year study duration.

Then, in the spirit of window shopping, I'll ask you to describe out loud what four years at Private Prestige would look like if money were no object. What's the dream college fantasy? Let's see how Solid State might deliver 75% of that experience at 25% of the cost.

Cost Isn't Everything!

I realize the bottom line price tag isn't everything. You still have passion, purpose, and pragmatism guiding your dreams! Surveys show the top criteria teens use are (Modern Campus, n.d.):

- 82%: Pursuing a career I'm interested in
- 81%: Learning real-world skills
- 79%: Earning potential long term
- 68%: Total cost and tuition
- 66%: Income immediately after graduation

These motivations are all super important in finding the right college fit. You need a program that aligns with your career aspirations and values, from job satisfaction to growth opportunities. Potential earnings afterward are critical, too. You want your investment to pay dividends! Dividends? Hmmm... Sounds familiar.

The college experience should equip you with skills that translate directly to workplace success, from critical thinking and analysis to networking, communication, and beyond.

Please end up somewhere you feel genuinely engaged in the subject matter, with professors guiding your professional development. Campus culture matters, too, from clubs and causes to life-long friendships. This is four years of nurturing your interests and growth!

Let's layer these criteria atop the cost comparisons to find your customized dream college recipe—tally up ratings for culture fit, alum outcomes, program alignment, and financials. Then, see which options are the best investment in your future goals and happiness!

PRIYA'S ULTIMATE CHOICE

Meet Priya; her passions are painting and environmental activism. After graduation, she dreams of turning her art into graphic design for change-making nonprofits.

Priya gets accepted to Santa Fe Art Academy and UMass Amherst for graphic design. Tuition is identical, but SFA would have higher loans for out-of-state living costs. Potential connections in the Santa Fe art scene draw her. However, UMass has a Design for Change Certificate she's interested in.

Priya weighs factors on a 1-5 scale:

Decision Factors	Santa Fe Art	UMass Amherst
Program Fit	4/5	5/5
School Culture	3/5	4/5
Campus Life	5/5	4/5
Total Cost/Debt	2/5	4/5
Location	5/5	3/5
Career Support	3/5	4/5
Academics	4/5	4/5
Graduates' Success	3/5	3/5
Teaching Quality	4/5	5/5
Personal Growth	5/5	4/5

As we can see from Priya's rating table above for her two top college choices, UMass Amherst edges out Santa Fe Art Academy after factoring everything from cost and program alignment to campus culture and projected career success after graduating.

Even though Santa Fe initially seemed more fun and aligned with Priya's artistic passions, quantifying each element made her reflect on long-term priorities. Saving money and having institutional career design support is what matters most for her goal of nonprofit graphic design. Assigning numerical ratings instead of fuzzy feelings helps optimize decision-making!

GOING CAR SHOPPING? DON'T JUST WINDOW SHOP!

I remember the utter thrill of buying my first car. But aside from shiny paint colors, we need to peel back the hood and kick the tires from a financial literacy angle! This ticket-item purchase must align with your budget and needs, not just desires. Let's ensure you research smartly.

Before rolling onto the lot, let's pause for some real talk. Owning wheels equals freedom, but also responsibility. Can you fill that tank long-term? Ask yourself:

- What are my must-have features? What's negotiable?
- How does this purchase fit my budget? Did I calculate insurance/gas/repairs?
- Can I realistically get financing—a loan approved from a bank—as a teen?

If you're financing:

- How could a cosigner impact my interest rate?
- Are first-time buyer programs best despite higher rates?
- What trade-offs come with each option?

When test driving:

- Am I comfortable in the driver's seat with good visibility?
- Is there enough cargo space for my lifestyle?
- How's the handling in realistic driving conditions?

When determining the budget:

- What income do I need to have to afford payments now and in the future?
- Am I choosing the most expensive car to impress others?
- How could picking a car above my means cripple future financial flexibility?

When comparing options:

- Did I rule out models truly beyond my current spending ability?
- Am I only looking at used cars, given depreciation realities?
- Have I researched insurance/gas/maintenance costs for each prospect?

Before deciding:

- Does this purchase align with both my wants AND calculated budget?
- Might this vehicle still stretch my dollars and cause money stress?
- Am I confident I can handle ongoing and unexpected costs of ownership?
- Did I leverage any pre-approvals to negotiate pricing?
- What additional fees are included? Can any be removed?
- Is this the best deal for my needs and wallet?

Asking these money questions upfront prevents buyer's remorse down the road! They'll steer you toward a sweet ride aligning with your budget and priorities. Keys to practicality and freedom!

When ready to make an offer, remember that negotiating can significantly lower pricing. First, research typical dealer margins across payment methods, invoice costs, financing rates, and incentives in your area. This equips you with leverage when asking for better financing terms, throwing in add-ons or bundles for free, or requiring dealers to remove pre-applied window tints charging $800! Let's hit the highway. What if they refuse to negotiate with you? Remember that you can walk away, they might change their mind, or you might find somewhere else that will negotiate.

A DREAM HOME... OR NOT

What does your dream house look like? White picket fence, modern marsh views, or a cozy city walk-up? Whether rental or forever must-own, envisioning what home represents in your adult life is exciting! But hold the housewarming party plans. Weighing the available options first allows us to make better decisions.

As teens on the cusp of adulthood, one of our first major life decisions is where we will live. Will we rent an apartment or go all in on buying our own starter home? It's exciting yet nerve-wracking to think about! While the best option depends on your unique situation, this choice positions you to embrace financial independence and responsibility. It's a tangible step toward shaping your future.

There are logical pros and cons to weigh when deciding whether to rent or buy, which we will explore. But also listen to your heart —what lifestyle aligns with this current chapter? Be true to your long-term financial goals as well as present needs.

Time for Some Internal Reflection:

Okay, we've examined the logical financial differences between the two options. Now let's go deeper:

- What stage of life are you entering in the next three years after high school? College? New job? Travel? Other goals?
- Does renting offer you more transitional flexibility to adapt to what's coming up versus buying?

- Are you someone who values constant change and new environments? Or thrives on stability?

Trust your intuition here! The objective facts only reveal so much. Rent or buy based on understanding who you are and what aligns with your current lifestyle. Revisit as life circumstances evolve. Discuss with your support system, like parents, mentors, and friends.

RENT VERSUS MORTGAGE

Are you tired of having roommates, dorm curfews, and your parents asking, "When are you coming home?" Well, picture this: Your place with no one to answer to! A space reflects your style; friends are welcome anytime, and you have total freedom.

Here's the deal, though: Banks offer special long-term loans called *mortgage loans* just for buying houses that cost way less per month than you'd guess. A mortgage lets you finance the upfront costs of a home you couldn't otherwise swing, paying back over many years.

I'm not dismissing the appeal of flexible renting life as you embark on young adult adventures. But real talk: Building assets for life-long security matters too sometimes. Ownership may be closer than you think if you are willing to budget tightly. That said, soul search what environment best complements your current priorities and personality.

Before making a final decision between renting and buying, here are vital questions to ask yourself:

- How prepared am I to handle repairs and maintenance costs for a home?
- Would I use and enjoy shared amenities that come with rentals?
- Am I ready to take on real estate taxes and insurance?
- Can I save enough for a full down payment on a house?
- How much do I value the flexibility to relocate elsewhere?
- Can I risk housing values decreasing after purchasing?
- Would I want to downsize from my owned home later in life?
- Would a predictable rent payment be easier to budget for now?
- How might insurance and utility costs compare renting vs buying?

Here's a quick comparison highlighting the pros and cons of renting and taking out a mortgage:

Renting an Apartment

Advantages	Disadvantages
No large upfront down payment is required (maybe small deposit)	Monthly rent payments can rise unexpectedly
Lower monthly costs like utilities	Can't customize paint, decor, layout
Avoid big surprise home repair expenses	Don't accrue equity over time like owners
Flexibility to relocate/move elsewhere	Restrictions on noise, guests, pets
Access to shared amenities	Less privacy depending on neighbors

Taking Out a Mortgage to Buy

Advantages	Disadvantages
Build equity in the home over time	Saving for a down payment is challenging
Tax deductions help lower costs	Must pay for all home repairs
Mortgage payments are stable over time	Can't quickly move somewhere new
Pride in customizing something owned	Must pay property taxes and insurance
No restrictions—pets, parties, etc.	Homeowners' insurance rates and property taxes may increase over time.
More privacy	Interest charges increase the total paid

SAVING FOR A HOME WHILE RENTING

You don't have to buy a home immediately, so don't worry if you want one but your financial situation doesn't allow it yet.

Janelle's Story

After four years of mentoring teens, I've seen bright 19-year-old Janelle work overtime while renting an apartment to set herself up to buy a small condo soon after finishing trade school. By budgeting diligently and minimizing spending, she has already saved $15K for a future down payment!

Her Tips for Fellow Teens:

1. Stash your cash in an online bank account that pays higher interest the more money you save—this keeps your home fund growing safely.
2. Create a budget that only spends on actual needs like food or gas to have more left to save each month. Get roommates to split the costs!

3. Pick up weekend/night side jobs delivering food or at the mall to make extra down payment savings money faster.

4. Instead of expensive Spring Break trips, tell your boss you can work extra hours over breaks for more home-buying dollars!

5. Become a resident assistant at college for accessible housing in exchange for planning dorm events and helping students out when issues happen. Bank that rent money saved!

6. Ask local banks about special programs to help first-time buyers your age with down payment money or lower mortgage rates.

7. Talk to community groups offering free money tips explaining how the home shopping process works and what banks look for when approving home loans.

8. Put any birthday gifts or graduation check money toward your future home, not splurging!

9. Look into safe investments like Bonds or CDs, where you earn a little extra interest cash on top of principal savings leftovers.

10. Stick to saving through smart budgeting moves no matter what. Soon, that diligence could land you a sweet pad to call your own!

SAVING FOR RETIREMENT

Where do you find yourself when you fantasize about your life in your 20s, 30s, or even 40s? Are you still stuck in the same job? No way. One day, you'll retire from work to chase other dreams. Plus, the earlier you start, the better. Why? Because retirement savings require serious money. So, what are *retirement savings?*

Retirement savings refers to money you put aside now, while you work, that you can use decades later to afford not working. Without these savings, you'd probably never be able to quit your job!

Contributing even slices of your pay to special accounts called *retirement accounts* invests that money and earns returns over decades. This allows your money to grow much faster through compound interest than just saving cash under your bed. For example, $100 contributed every month as a teenager could multiply to over $1 million by retirement age!

The key idea is that dedicated retirement accounts allow your money to work for you, automating growth through wise investments, so small amounts saved today transform into financial freedom later to pursue what truly makes you happy.

HOW MUCH DO YOU NEED TO SAVE?

Industry experts recommend having enough money saved to replace about 70-80% of the income you were earning from your job right before retirement. This allows you to maintain a similar lifestyle by withdrawing money from your retirement savings instead of counting on a paycheck.

For example, if you retire at 65 and make $100,000 annually at your job, you'd want $70-80K per year from your investment account. Without having that cushion, you may have to downgrade things like your home, travel budget, entertainment expenses, and more later on.

TYPES OF RETIREMENT ACCOUNTS

There are many ways to save for retirement. Still, a few popular account types you'll likely encounter include the *401(k)* and the *Individual Retirement Account (IRA),* which are of two kinds: the *Traditional IRA* and the *Roth IRA.*

RETIREMENT ACCOUNTS SECRET FORMULA

What if I told you there's a simple secret formula that can turn the $500 you squirrel away into your retirement account today into over $250,000 decades later without you lifting another finger? Seriously...

Here's how the math works:

First, you must open a retirement account. This allows you to start contributing parts of your paychecks or cash gifts, investing the money for decades.

These funds then get put into assets like stocks and bonds. Historically, these have paid average annual returns of around 7-8% back to investors over long time frames.

Now, here's where the real magic happens that can turn modest savings into a mountain of money down the road—compound interest!

Think of compound interest like a snowball gradually rolling down a mountain, picking up more mass and momentum as it keeps going. The longer it is untouched, the bigger it grows. It's the same idea with retirement savings over the years.

Your account gains interest not only on the dollars you contributed but also on the accumulated investment returns. You earn interest on interest!

For example, 16-year-old Ava contributed $50 to an IRA per month with a 7% yearly return. Just look at how that $50 monthly contribution can grow after 25 years thanks to compounding:

For year 1:

- Monthly contribution: $50
- Annual contribution: $600 (12 x $50)
- 7% interest on $600: 7/100 x $600 = $42
- Total at the end of Year 1: Amount + interest = $642

After 25 years of contributing, let's take a look at what Eva realizes:

Year	Monthly Contribution	Annual Contribution	Annual Interest (7%)	Total Balance
2025	$50	$600	$46	$1,932
2026	$50	$600	$49	$2,581
2030	$50	$600	$60	$5,205
2040	$50	$600	$100	$12,011
2045	$50	$600	$126	$15,588
2050	$50	$600	$187	$23,533

By the end of the 25th year, her retirement package will grow to $23,533!

The key is consistency and time. Start small and strive for regular contributions. Maintaining this disciplined saving into your 40s, 50s, and beyond lets compound interest take the wheel toward hitting big retirement savings targets.

How Do I Start Saving for Retirement?

Okay, you're convinced it's wise to start squirreling away money for later. But how do you begin? What's Step 1?

First, you'll want to open a retirement savings account. The two most common options are:

1. **401(k):** This account is offered directly through your workplace. A slice of each paycheck gets automatically deposited into investments. You can't miss what you never see, right? Some employers also contribute a percentage of your contributions—consider it a bonus. Be sure to ask your employers about this! Sometimes, they offer matches but don't advertise. There are tradition and Roth 401(k) plans. Generally, with a traditional plan you don't pay taxes on the money until you withdraw it during retirement. With a Roth account, you pay taxes on the money as you put it in instead. Do a little research to see which seems like a better fit for you.

2. **Individual Retirement Account:** You open this personal account separately, like through a bank or investment firm app. You manually move the money you earn into it regularly. This serves as a supplement to any workplace 401(k).

Next, you start contributing pieces of any money you earn into your chosen accounts. This can be paychecks if you have a formal job. Or cash from side hustles like dog walking, babysitting, and so on.

The key is opening any account ASAP and making consistent small contributions, especially with gift money or side job earnings.

Lastly, enable auto-transfers so retirement contributions happen seamlessly every time you get paid. Out of sight, out of mind! The ease helps stick to consistent saving in the long run.

Creating Your Future By Understanding Big Expenses

As we wrap up this crash course equipping you to balance dreams with dollars, here are the biggest takeaways so you can start adulting like a money boss:

When picking majors, dorms, cars, and apartments, tally every single cost to the penny over multiple years before locking in pricey commitments, got it? I'm arming you with secret formulas to reveal the full investment so impulse doesn't sabotage your future budget. Let's expose and then embrace reality!

Next—do some soul-searching when determining whether to rent or buy. Beyond the numbers, where will you thrive right now based on your priorities and personality amidst big life transitions? Quantify this for insight.

Want to retire a decade sooner than your friends? The secret formula shown to you turns tiny savings today into over $1 million later, thanks to something more powerful than magic... compound interest! Start now and thank me at 40.

Most importantly, you can absolutely turn passions into profitable careers and still afford sweet cars or vacations without accumulating oppressive debt. How? Get savvy through creative alternatives and pragmatic payment plans.

Call me your roadie; here to guide you confidently in balancing ambition with financial common sense! By following this blueprint built just for you, that first paycheck is only the beginning. Now go crush it!

CHAPTER ELEVEN

PROTECTING YOUR MONEY

Brace yourself—a new study shows teens fall for online scams at nearly 2,500% higher rates than just five years ago. Huge financial losses prove scammers targeting youth are getting way smarter (Westbrook, 2023).

In 2017, victims under 20 reported $8.2 million stolen by scams. By 2022, that number skyrocketed to a jaw-dropping $210 million as tricky schemes manipulate emotions and desires common in the teen experience (Westbrook, 2023). Fake influencer contests, shady gaming purchases, sketchy shopping sites, sextortion blackmail threats, and more are showing up in apps and sites popular with teens.

Once scammers access your personal information, it gets shared on hidden cyber-criminal networks, allowing identity theft for years. Being tech-savvy and guarded online is no longer enough to shield against increasingly slick scams.

Arming yourself to catch subtle red flags and lock down private info is crucial to avoid getting duped. This chapter reveals the most common scams fooling teens lately and breaks down expert tips to recognize shifty tactics and safeguard your details. Protecting your money now means more freedom to chase dreams later.

THEN VERSUS NOW

The internet provides awesome convenience—we can connect with friends, find entertainment, manage our money, and shop for anything imaginable worldwide. But expanded access also enables scammers to cast wider nets and anonymously target more victims than ever before. While past fraud centered on shady deals in person, the online world allows slick schemes on an unprecedented scale.

Just a generation ago, identity theft usually meant a stolen wallet, allowing limited damage by accessing a single bank account. One database breach can now expose millions' full names, birthdays, addresses, and social security numbers to sell on the dark web's black markets. $6.9 billion was lost to online scams in 2021 alone (Fletcher, 2023)!

Let's define fraud simply as deceit intended to make money illegally. Major categories relevant to online include:

Phishing/Smishing/Vishing

Phishing uses email, smishing uses text messages, and vishing uses phone calls to impersonate banks, businesses, government agencies, and even personal contacts you trust. They pretend there is some problem only you can urgently solve by clicking a link or sharing your login, credit card, or other sensitive details. Once entered on their fake sites, this confidential information gets stolen and used illegally.

Phishing messages can look amazingly credible, featuring logos and terminology identical to legitimate organizations. Be wary of any requests via email, text, or call for private data without independent confirmation of the senders' identities. To verify identities, find contact info through an official organization website or documentation and directly call them before providing any sensitive information.

Credit/Debit Card Fraud

Thieves steal credit/debit card data either through database hacking or skimmers secretly installed on ATM machines. Then, they use the numbers to make unauthorized, fraudulent purchases online or clone the cards to buy expensive goods they resell. Always check statements closely for mystery charges indicating potential card theft. Alert your bank or a credit card company promptly about suspicious activity to deactivate cards and reverse payments.

Remote Banking Fraud

Sophisticated phishing often targets bank login credentials using fake notifications of account issues that can only be resolved by inputting your username and password on very convincing, but fraudulent, sites that simply capture what you enter. Then, without physical cards, these online thieves transfer your money remotely into their own accounts, freshly opened under fake customer identities, impossible to track. Recovering such funds gets very tricky.

Identity Theft

Beyond losing money in existing accounts, stolen personal information also risks identity theft, where scammers open brand new lines of credit under your name and max them out without repayment. This tanks your credit score, and the unpaid debts fall on you to resolve. Regularly check for unauthorized credit applications filed using your social security number to catch them early and report identity theft quickly before it compounds disastrously. The credit apps have features that can help you perform these actions.

Advance Fee Fraud

Today, it's very common for scammers to post online ads promising hot investment opportunities, desirable purchases below market prices, or even lottery jackpots tied to overseas ventures. But they require upfront payment of taxes and fees first before you can claim the main money. Unfortunately, you never receive what was promised or hear from them again after you pay. It pays to verify strangers touting deals radically better than industry norms.

App Fraud

Phones are vulnerable to specially crafted malware when users download games or other software infected with hidden programs that monitor activity to steal usernames, passwords, and texts to access payment apps connected to your bank accounts. Always insist apps access only clearly relevant data to function properly, and read app permissions prompts closely to limit data vulnerability.

Account Takeover

Account takeover is when scammers access your existing financial accounts using stolen or hacked login credentials and passwords. Once inside, they can transfer funds out or make purchases just like legitimate account holders. Always use strong, unique passwords, enable two-factor authentication, and monitor transaction alerts for sudden account activity to minimize takeover.

Cyber Fraud

Cyber fraud refers to the illegal hacking of internet-connected systems, devices, and databases to access private data for financial crime. Beyond phishing's fake emails, cyber thieves deploy malware, viruses, ransomware, and hacking tools to break into protected networks to steal money, identities, or corporate information. Maintaining rigorous software security protocols at organizational levels is key to deterring mass data theft.

Ponzi Schemes

Ponzi schemes are elaborate investment scams named after the early 20th-century criminal *Charles Ponzi* (Probasco, 2023). They trick participants by claiming to deliver consistently high, guaranteed returns on money invested with no risk that is paid from later victims' cash infusions. Eventually, scammers disappear with all funds when the inflation of new investments can't keep pace with owed payouts. Scrutinize promised returns too good to be true.

Common Scams Used to Target Teens

Influencer impersonators leverage huge followers of popular figures by setting up fake accounts to sponsor contests, scholarships, or exclusive experiences. They require you to provide details or pay a fee before receiving any prize. Always verify an account's authenticity before engaging.

Romance scammers steal photos to create attractive dating profiles and shower affection on targets. After gaining trust, they fabricate emergencies requiring money. Reverse image search pictures or initiate video chats to confirm identities before developing feelings or providing funds.

With teens' high rates of smartphone sexting, **sextortion** has emerged as a devastating scam. Criminals pose as love interests online, exchange explicit images, and then threaten to make the photos public if blackmailed targets don't pay ransoms, tragically leading some to suicide. Never send compromising content to strangers.

Gaming purchases enable unlocking special features or advancing faster, but scammers trick gamers into handing over financial information and downloading malware without providing services paid for. Only transact through games' official stores.

Fake e-commerce sites offer hot products at unbelievable discounts, pocketing payments without sending items. Warning signs include grammatical errors, temporary email domains, absolutely no reviews, and prices too good to be true. Thoroughly vet sites before purchasing.

TIPS TO AVOID SCAMMERS

1. Watch out for too-good-to-be-true deals. If an offer seems too amazing to be real, it often is.
2. Research unfamiliar companies before providing personal information. Search "[company name] reviews" to see complaints.
3. Don't trust a company using a free email address like Gmail versus an official domain.
4. Misspellings and bad grammar on a website or email are major red flags.
5. If contacted by someone demanding quick action to avoid a fine or some other threat, pause. Scammers want to rush you before you detect lies.
6. Make sure online vendors have secure checkout, including "https" URLs. Avoid entering payment details on insecure sites.
7. When chatting online, be very wary of anyone who seems excessively eager to get personal fast without wanting to meet up.
8. Only download apps from official stores like Google Play and Apple App Store. Third-party app stores have looser security standards.
9. Always closely monitor bank and credit card statements to catch dodgy activity fast. Don't wait until the end of the month.
10. If an offer requests upfront payment to claim a prize or other too-good-to-be-true rewards, walk away. Legitimate contests never require you to pay to play.

THE IMPORTANCE OF PRIVACY AND SECURITY

What exactly is private data? It refers to personal details about you that you have the right to control access to. This includes information like your full name, date of birth, address, phone number, emails, browsing history, purchases, location data from your phone, and more.

Why does privacy matter? Handing data access to third parties puts you at major risk for issues like:

- **Identity theft:** Fraudsters can steal enough private info to pretend to be you and make purchases or open credit cards.
- **Financial loss:** Companies can sell or wrongly expose data that scammers leverage to drain bank accounts or trick you into paying for bogus services.
- **Reputation harm:** People's embarrassing or controversial emails, texts, and photos get hacked and published online every day. This causes public shame.

You work hard for money and status—privacy helps protect that! Here are tips to lock down personal data:

- Only share must-have details online and tweak security options on sites to hide anything extra.
- Never send money or super private data to strangers who contact you, demanding them urgently. Verify identities first.
- Install antivirus and malware protection software to block criminals from stealing data or spying via your device camera.

- Monitor bank and credit accounts daily for weird charges indicating possible identity theft. Act immediately if found.
- Use unique complex passwords on all accounts and turn on two-factor authentication when available.

The tips above empower you to enjoy web benefits while controlling exposure. Private wins the race! Value your dollars and self-respect enough to make privacy a priority. It will only gain relevance as life moves increasingly digital.

PREPARING YOURSELF FOR CHANGE

No matter where you are in your teen years, you've likely already witnessed how quickly aspects of society, technology, and culture can transform. Even in the past 5 years, how you engage with friends and information has probably shifted dramatically.

Change is clearly inevitable going forward as well. Many jobs that define the workforce 10 years from now don't even exist! And the latest social media platforms, video games, and devices that feel integral to daily life today may soon get abandoned as preferences evolve.

Reflect on trends, actions, and so on from your childhood that seem outdated now. That gap will only widen going forward in today's rapid-fire digital era. The job market continues evolving, too.

You must become comfortable adapting financial strategies as external factors shift constantly. The strategies enabling stability now likely won't serve the same way forever. Priorities will also pivot over time, influenced by new responsibilities and goals.

What does adaptability look like day-to-day? Simple things like:

- periodically reviewing budgets to reflect earnings increases and new expense needs.
- researching investing strategies maximizing growth for evolving market conditions.
- updating online privacy and security tactics as cybercrime techniques advance.
- learning new DIY money management tools to minimize reliance on advisors.

Flexibility needn't be intimidating! Consider more frequently: "How might I modify my approach if circumstances change?" This mental habit alone prepares your mindset to roll with change. Financial fluency in our era demands this agility.

A Brilliant Finish!

We did it! By now, you've completed the PRIME method and built an empowering foundation of essential money skills to last beyond your teens.

Let's recap the key lessons from each chapter tied to the PRIME steps:

- **Perceive:** We explored how your beliefs and assumptions about money fuel habits. Assessing these mindsets creates self-awareness for change.
- **Review:** You learned practical strategies to budget expenses, save consistently, and control spending aligned to personal priorities.

- **<u>I</u>nvest:** We unlocked earning potential by understanding banking, developing income sources, and putting savings to work in the market.
- **<u>M</u>obilize:** You defined financial goals for the future and crafted plans to target them. Building credit and managing debt were also covered.
- **<u>E</u>xercise:** Finally, we focused on safely adapting money skills as life evolves in our fast-paced, digital era.

By internalizing PRIME, you can recall helpful frameworks as future situations arise. The chapters also link together to reinforce that finance is profoundly personal. There is no generic path to stability—only what you deem worthwhile based on values.

Approach money decisions from this empowered perspective. Filter options through your identity and needs vs. outside pressures. Build flexibility to pivot approaches when circumstances change.

Most importantly, know that you are in control. Despite any challenges, the skills you possess pave the way to surmount obstacles and achieve security on your own terms. I'm proud of the financial independence and savvy you've gained. Congratulations on investing in yourself—it will pay dividends for years to come!

CONCLUSION

And there we have it—the end of the journey toward financial literacy through the *PRIME method* and its stepwise framework!

We captured a tremendous amount of information across 11 chapters ranging from personal money management concepts like planning budgets, building savings and understanding debt to investing basics, avoiding fraud, and more. I truly hope all the stories, data-backed insights, and actionable tips made financial comprehension more engaging.

Beneath the terminology and numbers lies a simple yet profound idea: Money profoundly shapes lives. Its impact links directly to the opportunities, stability, and peace accessible to us. And our savviness with personal finances determines those outcomes.

I aimed to clearly present frameworks, resources, and recommendations equipping you to make smart money moves aligned with your values. We covered everything from assessing deep-rooted money beliefs that influence behaviors to practical systems enabling consistent wealth building daily despite economic changes or setbacks.

Of course, numbers and percentages matter when making any financial decision. But the intentionality behind our goals and "why" we want financial freedom is much more. I hope your journey with this book connects earning, budgeting and investing back to your highest inspirations and potential for impact.

That inner spark matters most when choosing your path ahead amidst inevitable money crossroads and temporary failures. I'm honored to support the self-determination fueling your journey toward financial empowerment and adulthood. Please know my guidance will continue evolving alongside your needs, too!

I'd be overjoyed if you left an honest review sharing your biggest lessons learned or favorite chapters so that I can pay it forward by improving future money mentoring for teens. More than anything, please know your goals are within reach with focus and perseverance despite any money worries. You've so got this!

Now venture out into your financial destiny equipped to manage your finances with knowledge, and avoid hardships steering others off-course at your age. Stay determined in the face of challenges and patient through any early missteps. Your grit today transforms into peace and options tomorrow. Keep envisioning that future self living your boldest money dreams as motivation during difficult times!

Keeping the Game Alive

Now you have everything you need to Master Your Money, it's time to pass on your newfound knowledge and show other readers where they can find the same help. Simply by leaving your honest opinion of this book on Amazon, you'll show other stressed-out teens where they can find the information they're looking for, and pass their passion for Smart Money Moves forward.

Thank you for your help. The world of Money Skills for Modern Teens is kept alive when we pass on our knowledge – and you're helping Prosperity Books to do just that.

Scan the QR code below to leave your review.

Your review is like a beacon, guiding others through the exciting journey of mastering money. By sharing your thoughts, you're making a positive impact on fellow readers and helping them discover the secrets to financial success. So, go ahead, click that link, and let your voice be heard!

Thank you once again for being a part of our mission to make money skills accessible to everyone. Keep the game alive, and let's continue this journey together!

- Your fellow money mentor, Prosperity Books

GLOSSARY

401(k) account: A retirement savings account offered by employers allowing automatic contributions from paychecks, which may also include employer matches.

Automated teller machine (ATM): A computerized, self-serve kiosk that provides basic banking services when you insert your credit, debit, or ATM card.

Auto loan: A loan used to purchase a vehicle, often requiring a down payment and repaid in monthly installments.

Bad debt: Debt taken on to pay for items that won't generate income or increase in value.

Bank: A financial institution licensed to handle monetary transactions like accepting deposits, providing loans, and issuing credit.

Banking tools: Resources provided by banks to manage your money conveniently, including ATMs, online banking, mobile apps, and so on.

Bartering: Trading goods or services between parties without using money.

Bonds: Tradable, interest-bearing debt investments issued by governments and companies to fund operations.

Budget: An estimation of expected income and expenses used as a spending plan.

Business ownership: Possessing or starting a business by securing necessary financial resources, licenses, real estate, and so on.

CDs (Certificates of Deposit): A savings instrument often offered by banks guaranteeing returns after leaving deposits untouched for specified periods.

Checking account: A basic bank deposit account allowing withdrawals by check writing, ATM access, or debit card purchases tied to one's balance.

Collateral: An asset pledged to secure loan repayment if payments cannot be met.

Commodity money: Items that have value in themselves and can be directly exchanged for goods and services, like gold coins.

Compound interest: Interest calculated on both the initial principal of a deposit/loan and accumulated interest from preceding periods.

CPA (Certified Public Accountant): An accountant licensed by the state to file tax returns, conduct audits, and advise on business/individual financial decisions.

Credit history: An individual or business' past record of borrowing and repaying debts which influences credit score.

Credit report: A detailing of an individual or business credit-related information, like loan repayment behavior from various sources.

Credit score: A numeric assessment of one's creditworthiness to take on debt based on factors like repayment consistency.

Cryptocurrency: Decentralized digital money secured by cryptography and operating across distributed computing networks.

Custodial account: A bank account set up for and overseen by a legal guardian until a minor reaches legal age.

Cyber fraud: Illegal acts using the internet like data breaches, hacking, identity theft, and email scams intended to benefit from compromised information.

Debt: Money owed to lenders/creditors must be repaid, typically with added interest over time.

Digital money: Internet-based modes of instant payment like PayPal, Venmo, or Bitcoin, not tied to the physical cash exchange.

Discretionary expenses: Optional, non-essential spending on wants like recreation, entertainment, hobbies, and so on.

Diversification: Dividing investments among varied instruments and asset classes to reduce the overall risk profile.

Dividends: Portions of company profits paid out to stockholders either as cash or additional shares.

Down payment: An amount paid up front, typically to a lender, to make up the difference between the total price and financing provided for a large purchase.

Emergency fund: Savings put aside exclusively for unexpected financial crises or sudden loss of regular income stream.

Entrepreneurship: Identifying opportunities to meet consumer demands through new businesses, often assuming risks in organizing required resources and solutions.

Estate planning: Preparing for asset transfer upon incapacitation or death through legal wills, trusts, and so on.

ETFs (Exchange Traded Funds): Collections of various stocks or bonds combined into single diversified securities traded on exchanges.

Expenses: The money spent in exchange for goods or services, to fulfill basic needs or discretionary wants.

Filing taxes: Completing required annual tax paperwork reporting income, deductions, and credits to calculate the amount owed to or due from the government.

Financial goal: A defined milestone related to money management, like getting out of debt and saving up for college or retirement.

Financial literacy: Possessing knowledge and skills needed for effective personal money management decisions and resource utilization.

Financial plan: Long-term strategy and orderly approach towards achieving monetary objectives like wealth building or debt reduction.

Fiat money: Currency that lacks intrinsic value, declared as legal tender by governments, like most paper bills and coins.

Good debt: Debt taken to finance purchases expected to increase future value or income like homes, education, and businesses.

Gold standard: Backing currency with a fixed quantity of gold reserves to standardize value—rarely used today.

Health savings account (HSA): A special account allowing tax-advantaged savings earmarked specifically for current and future medical expenses.

Identity theft: The crime of obtaining private information to impersonate victims and make transactions or access funds through existing accounts fraudulently.

Income tax: Annual government tax levied on personal or business incomes after accounting for eligible tax reductions.

Installment loan: A loan repaid through equal amounts over fixed intervals for a defined time period via payment agreements.

Insured: Protection is guaranteed in exchange for premiums paid to limit financial losses from covered incidents, assets, or liabilities.

Interest rates: Percentages charged annually corresponding to used amounts, determining the cost of borrowing or gains from lending. Often you pay interest on money you borrow, but get paid interest on money you save.

Investing strategy: Plans guiding investment selection, amounts, timelines, and risk considerations based on individual constraints and return requirements.

Job: Regular employment position earning wages or salaries in exchange for defined work activities, outputs, or professional services rendered.

Loans: Money borrowed must be repaid over predefined periods according to amortization schedules or terms set by lenders.

Malware: Malicious software installed through tactics like phishing intended to infect devices and servers by attackers to breach privacy or demand ransom.

Marginal tax bracket: The highest tax rate at which your next dollar of earned income is taxed based on current income levels and defined thresholds.

Medical debt: Money owed to healthcare service providers like hospitals, doctors, or testing labs for costs not fully covered by insurance.

Mobile banking: Banking services like monitoring balances, transferring funds, or depositing checks are accessed conveniently via smartphones and mobile apps.

Mortgage: Long-term loans extended by banks to purchase real estate that serve as repayment guarantees through liens until amounts are fully paid off, including interest.

Mutual funds: Professionally managed investment funds pooled from many individual and institutional investors to purchase securities like bonds and stocks.

Online banking: Banking is conducted online via official bank websites or mobile applications rather than at physical branch locations.

Payroll tax: Taxes like social security automatically withheld from employee paychecks before receiving wages based on annual contribution requirements.

Peer-to-peer (P2P) payments: Direct lending deals and individual transactions, bypassing conventional financial institutions as intermediaries.

Phishing: Email fraud tactic meant to con users into sharing sensitive information by impersonating trustworthy entities like banks.

Planned purchases fund: An informal savings set aside for anticipated irregular large ticket predictable purchases like annually recurring insurance premiums.

Ponzi Schemes: Fraudulent investing scams promising unrealistic returns financed by cash infusions only from newer investors rather than legitimate earnings.

Precious metals: Rare commodity elements of recognized value like gold, silver, or platinum, often held as stores of value and for jewelry purposes.

Ransomware: Malware installed remotely to block access to files or systems until ransom amounts are paid, often in untraceable cryptocurrency transactions.

Real estate: Land, buildings, and attached natural resources that are tangible properties owned, lived in, or rented out to generate income.

Representative money: Indirect paper or digital monetary instruments representing the ability to readily exchange for fixed amounts of commodities or solutions kept in storage.

Residual Income: Earnings generated from work completed once that continue paying out over extended durations without ongoing active labor input.

Retirement account: Vehicles like IRAs, Roth IRAs, and 401(k)s invested in securities specifically to finance living costs post-ending active employment.

Retirement planning: The process of determining required total savings and making appropriate investment allocation decisions to prepare for effectively supporting yourself financially after retiring from the workforce.

Revolving debt: Flexible loan products like credit cards involving limits that don't require reapplying every single purchase and are centered on continuing usage and repayment over time.

Roth IRA: Retirement savings account allowing tax-free withdrawals subject to certain constraints for contributions made from post-tax income.

Simple interest: Calculating interest owed only on the principal amount rather than compounding previously earned interest.

Small business debt: Financing is obtained through SBA loans, business lines of credit, equipment financing, and credit cards to fund the operations of enterprises with less than 100 employees.

Smishing: Cyberattacks similar to phishing use mobile phone text or SMS messages rather than emails to extract sensitive user information illegally.

Standard deduction: A fixed dollar amount reducing the taxable income reported to IRS that filers can claim in lieu of calculating itemized deductions tallying exact qualified expenses.

Stock market: Exchanges enabling trading ownership in public companies through common shares investors can buy and sell seeking returns.

Student loan debt: Money students borrow to pay for academic degrees, expecting improved career prospects, enabling future repayment, but requiring payments shortly after graduation.

Tax: Mandatory contribution levied by governments on income, property sales, goods and services exchanges, used for funding national and regional infrastructure, and services.

Two-factor authentication: Improved login security mechanism needing users to provide account passwords and secondary credentials sent via calls, texts, or tokens.

Vishing: Phone scams similar to smishing using voice rather than text or video messages to collect sensitive personal or banking details by impersonating trusted organizations.

Wages: Compensation for labor or services provided, usually calculated based on hourly rates or annual salaries, and typically paid on recurring schedules via paychecks or direct bank deposits.

Withdraw: Taking deposited money like savings out from financial institutions or drawing down credit available on financing instruments like loans or lines of credit.

REFERENCES

Beattie, A. (2022, September 17). *The history of money: From barter to banknotes.* Investopedia. https://www.investopedia.com/articles/07/roots_of_money.asp

Board of Governors of the Federal System. (2021, May). *The Fed - Report on the economic well-being of U.S. households in 2020 - May 2021.* https://www.federalreserve.gov/publications/2021-economic-well-being-of-us-households-in-2020-dealing-with-unexpected-expenses.htm

Brainy Quotes. (n.d.-a). *Nicki Minaj quotes.* https://www.brainyquote.com/authors/nicki-minaj-quotes

Brainy Quotes. (n.d.-b). *Warren Buffet quotes.* https://www. brainyquote.com/quotes/warren_buffett_701497

Dickler, J. (2023a, August 8). *As credit card debt tops $1 trillion for the first time, "a huge test" for cardholders is coming.* CNBC. https://www.cnbc.com/2023/08/08/managing-student-loan-payments-as-credit-card-debt-tops-1-trillion.html

Dickler, J. (2023b, October 31). *62% of Americans are still living paycheck to paycheck, making it "The Main Financial Lifestyle," report finds.* CNBC. https://www.cnbc.com/2023/10/31/62percent-of-americans-still-live-paycheck-to-paycheck-amid-inflation.html

Epperson, S., & Dhue, S. (2023, April 11). *70% of Americans are feeling financially stressed, new CNBC survey finds.* CNBC. https://www.cnbc.com/2023/04/11/70percent-of-americans-feel-financially-stressed-new-cnbc-survey-finds.html

Fletcher, L. (2023, October 2). *US sees alarming surge in online scams targeting kids and teens, study shows.* WJLA. https://wjla.com/features/i-team/united-states-scams-kids-teens-social-media-online-facebook-whats-app-instagram-prevention-scammer-nigeria-419-yahoo-boy-fraud-fake-profiles-seniors-safety-money-social-catfish

Gillespie, L. (2023, September 18). *Survey: 48% of social media users have impulsively purchased a product seen on social media.* Bankrate. https://www.bankrate.com/personal-finance/social-media-survey/

Goodreads. (n.d.). *A quote by Kung Fu Panda.* https://www.goodreads.com/quotes/2896447-oogway-there-are-no-accidents-shifu-sighs-yes-i-know

Kumar, R. (2014). *Gold standard.* Science Direct. https://www.sciencedirect.com/topics/economics-econometrics-and-finance/gold-standard

Marder, A. (2023, May 30). *Most Americans have a monthly budget, but many still over-*

spend. Nerd Wallet. https://www.nerdwallet.com/article/finance/data-2023-budgeting-report

Martin, H. D. (2023, November 28). *Mainewhile: Budgets reflect values – How are we doing?* Press Herald. https://www.pressherald.com/2023/11/28/mainewhile-budgets-reflect-values-how-are-we-doing/#:~:text=This%20senti-ment%20was%20put%20far

Modern Campus. (n.d.). *Are you sharing the data teens need to choose your college?* Modern Campus. https://moderncampus.com/blog/are-you-sharing-the-data-teens-need-to-choose-your-college.html

Perez, S. (2020, December 30). *EarlyBird's new app lets families and friends gift' investments to children*. TechCrunch. https://techcrunch.com/2020/12/30/early birds-new-app-lets-families-and-friends-gift-investments-to-children/

Probasco, J. (2023, February 28). *Who was Charles Ponzi? What did he create?* Investopedia. https://www.investopedia.com/who-is-charles-ponzi-5216783

Reinicke, C. (2022, June 1). *54% of teenagers feel unprepared to finance their futures, survey shows.* CNBC. https://www.cnbc.com/2022/06/01/54percent-of-teens-feel-unprepared-to-finance-their-futures-survey-shows.html

Schulz, M. (2020, October 8). *44% of Americans plan to apply for store Credit Card this holiday.* LendingTree. https://www.lendingtree.com/credit-cards/study/store-credit-card-report/

Sowa, E., Campbell, M., & Cohen, B. (2019, November 12). *14-year-old Alina Morse invents all-natural candy that cleans your teeth.* ABC7 San Francisco. https://abc7news.com/alina-morse-zollipops-candy-healthy/5672130/

Tepper, T. (2021, July 6). *Acorns review 2021.* Forbes Advisor. https://www.forbes.com/advisor/investing/acorns-review/

Turner, T. (2023, February 3). *47+ fascinating financial literacy statistics in 2022.* Annuity. https://www.annuity.org/financial-literacy/financial-literacy-statistics/

United States Mint. (n.d.). *Fort Knox bullion depository.* https://www.usmint.gov/about/mint-tours-facilities/fort-knox

U.S. Chamber of Commerce. (2019, October 21). *Becoming the boss: Meet the mini-mogul making bow ties fashionable again.* https://www.uschamber.com/co/good-company/growth-studio/mos-bows-founder-moziah-bridges

Westbrook, E. (2023, October 24). *Top 3 online scams teens and parents should know about -- Plus, how to avoid them.* CBS News. https://www.cbsnews.com/newyork/news/top-3-online-scams-teens-and-parents-should-know-about-plus-how-to-avoid-them/

Zaleski, A. (2023, March 29). *Convincing Gen Z to work in the Federal Government.* Washington Post. https://www.washingtonpost.com/business/2023/03/29/more-federal-internships/

www.ingramcontent.com/pod-product-compliance
Lightning Source LLC
Chambersburg PA
CBHW051428130726
47987CB00005B/1956